D1323544

ISBN: 9781314610833

Published by:
HardPress Publishing
8345 NW 66TH ST #2561
MIAMI FL 33166-2626

Email: info@hardpress.net
Web: http://www.hardpress.net

THE COLLECTED WORKS OF
HENRIK IBSEN

VOLUME III

BRAND

THE COLLECTED WORKS OF
HENRIK IBSEN

Copyright Edition.   Complete in 11 Volumes.
Crown 8vo, price 4s. each.

ENTIRELY REVISED AND EDITED BY
WILLIAM ARCHER

LONDON: WILLIAM HEINEMANN,
21 BEDFORD STREET, W.C.

THE COLLECTED WORKS OF
HENRIK IBSEN

COPYRIGHT EDITION

VOLUME III

BRAND

TRANSLATED AND WITH INTRODUCTION BY

C. H. HERFORD, Litt.D., M.A.

LONDON
WILLIAM HEINEMANN
1912

First printed (small 4to, 7s 6d) . January 1894
New Impressions . *October* 1898, *March* 1903

COLLECTED EDITION

First printed . . . . *November* 1906
New Impressions . *December* 1908, *May* 1912

2 50

CONTENTS

Translated by C. H. HERFORD

BRAND.

INTRODUCTION.[1]

BRAND was written in the summer of 1865, at Ariccia, near Rome. Fifteen months before, Ibson had left Christiania, a voluntary exile, eager to escape from the narrow Scandinavian world, and burning with the sense of national disgrace Denmark was in the throes of the heroic but hopeless struggle to which her northern kinsmen had sent only a handful of volunteers. He had travelled southward, almost within hearing of the Prussian guns ; and among the passengers on the steamer was that venerable silver-haired mother who, as his sarcastic verses tell, believed so firmly in the safety of her soldier-son, and with such good ground, " for he was a *Norwegian* soldier."[2] On arriving at Rome he turned resolutely away from these rankling memories, broke all the bonds that tied him to his country, plunged into the study of the ancient world, and made preparation for

---

[1] For a more detailed discussion of *Brand* the reader may be referred to the Introduction prefixed to the original edition of the present translation (London, 1894).

[2] The poem *Troens grund.* It is translated by Mr. Wicksteed, *Lect.* p. 24. This admirable little volume is indispensable to the English student of Ibsen's poetry.

that colossal drama on the Emperor Julian which
eight years later saw the light.

But the genius of the North held him in too
strong a grip. "Never have I seen the Home
and its life so fully, so clearly, so near by," he
told the Christiania students in 1873, "as precisely
from a distance and in absence."[1] Under the
Italian sky, among the myrtles and aloes of the
"Paradise of exiles," there rose before him more
vividly than ever the vision of the stern and
rugged Norwegian landscape, the solemn twilight of
the fjord, the storm-swept glacier, the peasant-folk
absorbed in the desperate struggle for bread, official-
dom absorbed in material progress, "intelligence"
growing refined, "humane," and somewhat effeminate ;
and, emerging here and there, glimpses somewhat
futile and forlorn of heroic manhood. A summer
tour which he had made among the western fjords in
July 1862, on a commission from Government to
collect popular legends, supplied a crowd of vivid local
and personal reminiscences ; a ruined parsonage
under a precipice, a little mouldering church, a wild
march across Jotunheim in storm and snow, and then
the dizzy plunge down into one of those deep lowland
valleys that strike up like huge rocky rifts from the
fjord-head into the heart of the mountains. A few
months of intense labour sufficed to organise these
scattered images into a moving world of drama,
penetrated through and through with Ibsen's
individuality, and clothed in rich and many-coloured
poetry. He had as yet written nothing at once so
original, so kindling, and so profusely strewn with
the most provocative brilliances of style ; nothing

[1] Speech to the students, printed in full in Halvorsen, *Norsk
Forfatter-lexikon*, art. "Ibsen."

which, with all its fierce invective against Norway, was so profoundly and intimately Norwegian in colouring and in spirit. Upon its publication, on March 15, 1866, at Copenhagen, the whole Scandinavian world was taken by storm.

The sale was from the outset immense, and has continued, though at a diminished pace, till the present day. Four editions appeared before the close of 1866 ; the eleventh in 1889. Ibsen was little accustomed to such success. It is said that immediately after the publication his sister-in-law drank to the " tenth edition " ; the poet confidently shook his head and declared that the profits of the tenth edition should be hers. She took him at his word, and has not repented her prophetic gift.[1] Outside Scandinavia, too, the name of the author of *Brand* rapidly became famous. It was the beginning of his European fame. In Germany, its intellectual suggestiveness and philosophical mysticism were keenly appreciated ; it was compared with *Hamlet* and with *Faust*. No less than four translations appeared there between 1872 and 1882.

Even on the stage, for which it was never meant, *Brand* has not been quite unknown. In Christiania the Fourth Act has repeatedly been played ; but it was reserved for the Director of the New Theatre at Stockholm, L. Josephson, to undertake the bold experiment of performing the whole. On March 24, 1885, a crowded house sat through a performance which lasted from 6.30 to 1.15. It was repeated fifteen times.[2]

[1] Halvorsen, *Forfatter-lexikon*, u.s.

[2] The Stockholm *Ny ill. Tidning*, 1885, Nos. 14, 15, gives an interesting account of the performance, with several illustrations. *Brand* was played by E. Hillberg. Ibsen congratulated the Director in a letter printed by Halvorsen, *u.s.*

In 1893 a single performance of the Fourth Act, in the present version, was given in London.

Together with its still more splendid and various, yet completely dissimilar successor, *Peer Gynt, Brand* marks an epoch in Scandinavian literature   A large majority of those who know the original believe that it marks an epoch in the literature of Europe. Nothing in English literature in the least resembles a work, which is nevertheless peculiarly fitted to impress and to fascinate the English nature.[1]   But those who can imagine the prophetic fire of Carlyle fused with the genial *verve* and the intellectual athleticism of Browning, and expressed by aid of a dramatic faculty to parallel which we must go two centuries backward, may in some degree understand that fascination.

Primarily, however, *Brand* was addressed to Norway and to Norway alone.   It was the passionate cry—at once invective and appeal—of a Norwegian, to the mother-country, of which, grievous as her failings are, he cannot bring himself to despair.   The situation must be recalled.   When the Danish King, in November 1863, supported by the King of Sweden, declared Slesvig an integral part of Denmark, there was much loud jubilation in Norway at the extension of " Scandinavian " rule, even among people not at all prepared to allow that the cause of Denmark and of Norway were one ;   while the more ardent spirits pledged themselves over flowing cups to support their " brothers " in the field.   The actual invasion of Denmark by Prussia and Austria which followed (February 1864) was, in Ibsen's eyes, for

[1] Mr. Gosse has, however, pointed out that it has points of likeness, striking rather than important, to Dobell's dramatic poem *Balder* (1854).

his own country too, a moral crisis which could be manfully met only in one way ; and when the Storthing, by virtually refusing war,[1] forced the King, to his bitter shame, to leave Denmark to her fate, Ibsen's heroic scorn broke into flame, and found its fiercest and keenest expression in the invectives of his hero, Brand.

Brand was no doubt originally intended to be simply an embodiment of Ibsen's own heroic ideal of character. He is represented as a priest of modern Norway. But Ibsen has himself declared that this was not at all essential for his purpose. " I could have applied the whole syllogism just as well," he told Georg Brandes, " to a sculptor, or a politician, as to a priest. I could quite as well have worked out the impulse which drove me to write, by taking Galileo, for instance, as my hero—assuming, of course, that Galileo should stand firm and never concede the fixity of the earth ;—or you yourself in your struggle with the Danish reactionaries."[2] The gist of the whole is therefore ethical, in spite of its theological clothing, and in spite of the theological phraseology in which Ibsen's own ethical conceptions were as yet habitually entangled. The faith which inspires it is the faith in the spirit of man—" the one eternal thing," as Brand declares in a splendid outburst, that of which churches and creeds are only passing moods, and which, now dispersed and disintegrated among the torsos of humanity, shall one day gather once more into a whole.

Brand was to be the ideal antitype of the Nor-

---

[1] They accepted the King's demand that the army should be placed absolutely in his hands, but coupled the condition that he was to make war only in alliance with England or France.

[2] First published by Brandes in his *Gjennembrudtsmænd;* partially quoted by Jæger, *H. Ibsen* (Eng. Tr. p. 155).

wegian people. But Ibsen's own complexity of
nature, and perhaps also his keen dramatic instinct
interfered with this simple scheme. The ideal type
grew human and individual; the Titan going forth
with drawn sword against the world became a
struggling and agonised soul, swayed by doubts and
entangled by illusion; the vices he denounces are
represented by men, drawn mostly with a genial and
humorous, and, in the case of the "humane" old
Doctor, with a kindly and sympathetic hand. The
beautiful creation of Agnes serves the purpose of
satire admirably in the Second Act, where her
heroism is set off against the "faintheartedness" of
the Peasants and Einar; but in the Third and Fourth
Acts she has passed into the domain of tragedy; her
heroism is no longer an example hurled at the cring-
ing patriots of 1864, but a pathetic sacrifice to the idol
which holds her husband in its spell. Thus the
tragedy of Brand, the man, struggling in the grip of
his formula, disengages itself from the "satire" of
Brand, the Titan, subduing the world to his creed.

Brand is written throughout in one or other of two
varieties of four-beat verse. "I wanted a metre
in which I could career where I would, as on horse-
back," Ibsen said to the present translator in 1893.
And in his hands the metre develops a versatility of
tone, rhythm and rhyme arrangement for which
Browning's *Christmas Eve and Easter Day* is the only
proximate English parallel. But the two varieties—
iambic and trochaic, instead of being deftly
mingled, as in *L'Allegro* and *Il Penseroso*, are kept
strictly apart and used with felicitous effect to
heighten the distinction between two classes of scene.
The iambic is the measure of the more familiar and

pedestrian scenes, where the tone is colloquial, argumentative, satirical, or, again, bustling and lively. The swifter and more sensitive trochaic, on the other hand, is used in scenes of passion and poetry, of poignant emotion, of mystic vision, of solitary thought. Thus all the great revealing crises of the action, the points at which the informing fire breaks through—the monologues of Brand, the visions of Agnes (Acts II. v.), and the scenes in which they successively "stand at the crossway" to choose (end of Acts II. III. IV.)—are conveyed in the more lyrical metre, while the more conversational clothes the intervening tracts of common life.[1]

The present translation retains the metres of the original, and follows the text, in general, line for line. But no attempt has been made at exact correspondence in points, such as the use of single or double rhymes, and the sequence and arrangement of rhymes, where the original itself is completely arbitrary.

[1] In Spain, conversely, the trochaic was the normal metre, the iambic a comparatively rare variation in situations of exceptional dignity.

P|

BRAND

(1865)

A

PERSONS REPRESENTED.

BRAND.
HIS MOTHER.
EINAR, *a painter.*
AGNES.
THE MAYOR.
THE DOCTOR.
THE DEAN.
THE SEXTON.
THE SCHOOLMASTER.
GERD.
A PEASANT.
HIS YOUNG SON.
ANOTHER PEASANT.
A WOMAN.
ANOTHER WOMAN.
A CLERK.
PRIESTS AND OFFICIALS.
CROWD : MEN, WOMEN AND CHILDREN.
THE TEMPTER IN THE DESERT.
THE INVISIBLE CHOIR.
A VOICE.

The action takes place in our own time, at various points around a fjord-hamlet on the west coast of Norway.

BRAND.

ACT FIRST.

High up in the mountain snowfields. The mist lies thick and close ; it is raining, and nearly dark

BRAND in black, with stick and wallet, is struggling on westward. A PEASANT AND HIS YOUNG SON, who have joined him, are a little way behind.

THE PEASANT.
[*Calling after* BRAND.]
Hullo, you stranger fellow, stay !
Where are you ?

BRAND.
Here !

THE PEASANT.
You've got astray !
The fog's so thick, my sight it passes
To see a staff's-length 'fore or back——

THE SON.
Father, here's clefts !

THE PEASANT.
And here crevasses !

BRAND.

And not a vestige of the track.

THE PEASANT.
[*Crying out.*]
Hold, man!   God's death—!   The very ground
Is but a shell!   Don't stamp the snow!

BRAND.
[*Listening.*]
I hear the roaring of a fall.

THE PEASANT.
A beck has gnawed its way below;
Here's an abyss that none can sound;
'Twill open and engulf us all!

BRAND.
As I have said, I must go on.

THE PEASANT.
That's past the power of any one.
I tell you—the ground's a rotten crust—
Hold, hold, man!   Death is where it's trod

BRAND.
A great one gave me charge; I must.

THE PEASANT.
What is his name?

BRAND.
His name is God.

THE PEASANT.
And what might you be, pray?

BRAND.

A priest.

THE PEASANT.

Maybe ; but one thing's clear at least ;
Though you were dean and bishop too
Death will have laid his grip on you
Ere daybreak, if you dare to breast
The glacier's cavern-cloven crest.
　　[Approaching warily and insinuatingly.]
Hark, priest, the wisest, learned'st man
Cannot do more than what he can.
Turn back ; don't be so stiff and stout !
A man has but a single life ;—
What has he left if that goes out ?
The nearest farm is two leagues off,
And for the fog, it's thick enough
To hack at with a hunting-knife.

BRAND.

If the fog's thick, no glimmering ray
Of marsh-light lures our feet astray.

THE PEASANT.

All round lie ice-tarns in a ring,
And an ice-tarn's an ugly thing.

BRAND.

We'll walk across.

THE PEASANT.

On waves you'll walk !

Your deeds will hardly match your talk.

BRAND.

Yet one has proved,—whose faith is sound
May walk dry-footed on the sea.

THE PEASANT.

Yes, men of olden time, maybe;
But nowadays he'd just be drowned.

BRAND.
[*Going.*]

Farewell!

THE PEASANT.
You throw your life away!

BRAND.

If God should haply need its loss,——
Then welcome chasm, and flood, and foss.

THE PEASANT.
[*To himself.*]
Nay, but his wits are gone astray!

THE SON.
[*Half-crying.*]
Come away, Father! see how black
With coming tempest is the wrack!

BRAND.
[*Stopping and approaching again*]
Hear, peasant; you at first profess'd,
Your daughter by the fjordside lying,
Had sent you word that she was dying,
But could not with a gladsome breast,
Until she saw you, go to rest?

THE PEASANT.
That's certain, as I hope for bliss!

BRAND.
And as her last day mentioned—this?

THE PEASANT.

Yes.

BRAND.

Not a later ?

THE PEASANT.
No.

BRAND.

Then come

THE PEASANT.
The thing's impossible—turn home !

BRAND.
[*Looking fixedly at him.*]
Listen !   Would you give twenty pound
If she might have a blest release ?

THE PEASANT.
Yes, parson !

BRAND.
Forty ?

THE PEASANT.
House and ground
I'd very gladly sign away
If so she might expire in peace !

BRAND.
But would you also give your life ?

THE PEASANT.
What ? life ?   My good friend——— !

BRAND.
Well ?

THE PEASANT.
[*Scratching his head.*]
Nay, nay,
I draw the line somewhere or other——!
In Jesus' name, remember, pray,
At home I've children and a wife.

BRAND.
He whom you mention had a mother.

THE PEASANT.
Ay, that was in the times of yore;—
Then marvels were of every day;
Such things don't happen any more.

BRAND.
Go home.   You travel in death's track.
You know not God, God knows not you.

THE PEASANT.
Hoo, you are stern!

THE SON.
[*Pulling him away.*]
Come back! come back

THE PEASANT.
Ay, ay; but he must follow too!

BRAND.
Must I?

THE PEASANT.
Ay, if I let you bide
Up here in this accursed weather,
And rumour told, what we can't hide,
That you and we set out together,
I'm haul'd some morning to the dock,—

And if you're drown'd in flood and fen,
I'm sentenced to the bolt and lock——

BRAND.

You suffer in God's service, then.

THE PEASANT.

Nor his nor yours is my affair ;
My own is hard enough to bear.
Come then !

BRAND.

Farewell !
    [*A hollow roar is heard in the distance.*

THE SON.

[*Shrieking.*]

          An avalanche roar !

BRAND.

[*To the* PEASANT *who has seized his collar.*]
Off !

THE PEASANT.

    Nay !

BRAND.

This instant !

THE SON.

        Stay no more !

THE PEASANT.

[*Struggling with* BRAND.]
Nay, devil take me——— !

BRAND.

[*Shakes him off and throws him down in the snow.*]
        That, depend
On it, he will do in the end !   [*Goes.*

THE PEASANT.

[Sitting and rubbing his arm.]

Ow, ow ; his arm's an iron rod ;
And that's what he calls serving God
                [Calling as he gets up.]
Ho, priest !

THE SON.

He's gone athwart the hill.

THE PEASANT.

Ay, but I see him glimmer still.
            [Calling again.]
Hear me,—if you remember, say,
Where was it that we lost the way ?

BRAND.

[In the mist.]

You need no cross to point you right ;—
The broad and beaten track you tread.

THE PEASANT.

God grant it were but as he said,
And I'd sit snug at home to-night.
            [He and his Son retire eastwards.

BRAND.

*[Reappears higher up, and listens in the direction in
which the* PEASANT *went.]*

Homeward they grovel ! Thou dull thrall,
If but thy feeble flesh were all,
If any spark of living will
Sprang in thee, I had help'd thee still.
With breaking back, and feet way-worn,
Lightly and swift I had thee borne ;—

But help is idle for the man
Who nothing wills but what he can.
                    [*Goes further on.*]
Ah life! ah life!   Why art thou then
So passing sweet to mortal men?
In every weakling's estimation
His own life does as grossly weigh
As if the load of man's salvation
Upon his puny shoulders lay.
For every burden he's prepared,
God help us,—so his life be spared!
                    [*Smiles as in recollection.*]
Two thoughts in boyhood broke upon me,
And spasms of laughter in me woke,
And from our ancient school-dame won me
Many a just and bitter stroke.
An Owl I fancied, scared by night;
A Fish that had the water-fright;
I sought to banish them;—in vain,
They clung like leeches to my brain.
Whence rose that laughter in my mind?
Ah, from the gulf, dimly divined,
Between the living world we see
And the world as it ought to be,
Between enduring what we must,
And murmuring, it is unjust!
    Ah, whole or sickly, great or small,
Such owls, such fishes, are we all.
Born to be tenants of the deep,
Born to be exiles from the sun,
This, even this, does us appal;
We dash against the beetling steep,
Our starry-vaulted home we shun,
And crying to heaven, bootless pray
For air and the glad flames of day!
                    [*Pauses a moment, starts, and listens.*]

What do I hear?   A sound of singing.
Ay, blended song and laughter ringing.
With now a cheer and now a hollo,—
Another—and another—follow !
   Lo, the sun rises ; the mist lifts.
Already through the breaking rifts
The illimitable heights I see ;
And now that joyous company
Stands out against the morning light
Upon the summit of the height.
Their shadows taper to the west,
Farewells are utter'd, hands are pressed.
And now they part, the others move
Eastward away, two westward wend,
And, waving hats and kerchiefs, send
Their farewell messages of love.

      [*The sun gradually breaks through and dis-*
         perses the mist. BRAND *stands and looks*
         down on the two as they approach.]

How the light glitters round these two !
It is as if the mist took flight,
And flowering heather clothed the height,
And heaven laugh'd round them where they go.
Brother and sister, hand in hand,
They spring along the hill together,
She scarcely stirs the dewy heather,
And he is lissome as a wand.
Now she darts back, he rushes after,
Now slips aside, eludes his aim,—
Out of their gambols grows a game——!
And hark, a song out of their laughter !

      [EINAR *and* AGNES, *in light summer dress,*
         both of them warm and glowing, come
         playing across the level. The mist is gone;
         a bright summer morning lies on the
         mountains.]

Einar.

Agnes, my beautiful butterfly,
Playfully shalt thou be caught !
I am weaving a net, and its meshes fine
Are all of my music wrought !

Agnes.

[*Dancing backwards and always eluding him.*]
And am I a butterfly, dainty and slight,
Let me sip of the heather-bell blue,
And art thou a boy, let me be thy sport,
But oh ! not thy captive too !

Einar.

Agnes, my beautiful butterfly,
I have woven my meshes so thin,
And never availeth thy fluttering flight,
Soon art thou my captive within.

Agnes.

And am I a butterfly young and bright,
Full joyously I can play,
But if in thy net I a captive lie
Oh, touch not my wings, I pray !

Einar.

Nay, I will lift thee with tender hand,
And lock thee up in my breast,
And there thou shalt play thy whole life long
At the game thy heart loves best.
[*They have unwittingly approached a sheer
precipice, and are now close to the edge.*

Brand.

[*Calls down to them.*]
Hold ! hold ! You stand by an abyss !

EINAR.

Who calls us ?

AGNES.

[*Pointing up.*]
See !

BRAND.

           Heed where you go
Your feet are on the hollow snow
That overhangs a precipice.

EINAR.

[*Clasping her, and laughing up to* BRAND.]
Needless for her and me your fears !

AGNES.

We have a whole life long to play !

EINAR.

In sunshine lies our destined way,
And ends but with a hundred years.

BRAND.

And then you perish ? So !

AGNES.

[*Waving her veil.*]
           No; then
We fly to heaven and play again !

EINAR.

A hundred years to revel given,
Each night the bridal lamps aflame,—
A century of glorious game——

BRAND.

And then—?

EINAR.

Then home again to heaven,—

BRAND.

Aha! so that is whence you came?

EINAR.

Of course; how should we not come thence?

AGNES.

That is, our very latest flight
Is from the valley, eastward hence.

BRAND.

I think I saw you on the height.

EINAR.

Ay, it was there on those loved faces
Even but now we look'd our last,
And with clasp'd hands, kisses, embraces
Seal'd all our tender memories fast!
Come down to us, and I will tell
How God's been good beyond compare—
And you shall all our gladness share——!
Pooh, stand not like an icicle!
Come, thaw now! There, I like you so.
First, I'm a painter, you must know,
And even this to me was sweet,—
To lend my fancy wings and feet,
In colours to bid life arise,
As He of grubs breeds butterflies.
But God surpass'd Himself when He
My Agnes gave me for my bride!
I came from travels over sea,
My painter's satchel at my side——

AGNES.

[*Eagerly.*]

Glad as a king, and fresh, and free,—
And knew a thousand songs beside!

EINAR.

Just as the village I pass'd through,
She chanced to dwell an inmate there.
She longed to taste the upland air,
The scented woods, the sun, the dew;
Me God unto the mountains drew,—
My heart cried out: Seek Beauty's might
In forests dim and rivers bright
And flying clouds beneath the blue.—
Then I achieved my height of art:
A rosy flush upon her cheek,
Two joyous eyes that seem'd to speak,
A smile whose music filled the heart—

AGNES.

For you, though, all that art was vain,
You drank life's beaker, blind and rapt,
And then, one sunny morn, again
Stood, staff in hand and baggage strapp'd—

EINAR.

Then suddenly the thought occurr'd:
"Why, friend, the wooing is forgot!"
Hurrah! I ask'd, she gave her word,
And all was settled on the spot.
Our good old doctor, like a boy,
Was all beside himself with joy;
So three whole days, and whole nights three,
Held revelry for her and me;
Mayor and constable, clerk and priest,—
All the grown youth was at the feast.

Last night we left, but not for that
The revel or the banquet ceased ;
With banner'd pole and wreathed hat,
Up over bank, on over brae,
Our comrades brought us on our way.

AGNES.

The mountain-side we danced along,
In couples now, and now in groups,—

EINAR.

Drank luscious wine from silver stoups,—

AGNES.

Awoke the summer night with song,—

EINAR.

And the thick mist before our feet
Beat an obsequious retreat.

BRAND.

And now your way lies— ?

EINAR.

To the town
Before us.

AGNES.

To my parents' home.

EINAR.

First over yonder peak, then down
To the fjord haven in the west ;
On Egir's courser through the foam
Ride homeward to the bridal feast,—
So to the sunny south together
Like paired swans in their first flight——

III   B

BRAND.

And there——— ?

EINAR.

A life of summer weather,
A dream, a legend of delight.
For on this Sabbath mōrn have we,
High on the hills, without a priest,
From fear and sorrow been released
And consecrated to gaiety.

BRAND.

By whom ?

EINAR.

By all the merry crowd.
With ringing glasses every cloud
Was banish'd that might dash the leaves
Too rudely at our cottage eaves.
Out of our speech they put to flight
Each warning word of stormy showers,
And hail'd us, garlanded with flowers,
The true-born children of Delight.

BRAND.
[Going.]

Farewell, ye two.

EINAR.
[Starting and looking more closely at him.]
I pray you, hold
Something familiar in your face———

BRAND.
[Coldly.]

I am a stranger.

EINAR.

Yet a trace
Surely there lingers of an old
Friend of my school-days—

BRAND.

School-friends, true;
But now I am no more a boy.

EINAR.

Can it be—— ?
[*Cries out suddenly.*]
Brand ! It is ! O joy !

BRAND.

From the first moment I knew you.

EINAR.

Well met ! a thousand times well met !
Look at me !—Ay, the old Brand yet,
Still centred on the things within,
Whom never any one could win
To join our gambols.

BRAND.

You forget
That I was homeless and alone.
Yet you at least I loved, I own.
You children of the southern land
Were fashion'd of another clay
Than I, born by a rocky strand
In shadow of a barren brae.

EINAR.

Your home is here, I think ?

BRAND.
My way
Lies past it.

EINAR.
Past? What, further?

BRAND.
Far
Beyond, beyond my home.

EINAR.
You are
A priest?

BRAND.
[*Smiling.*]
A mission-preacher, say.
I wander like the woodland hare,
And where I am, my home is there.

EINAR.
And whither is your last resort?

BRAND.
[*Sternly and quickly.*]
Inquire not!

EINAR.
Wherefore?

BRAND.
[*Changing his tone.*]
Ah,—then know,
The ship that stays for you below
Shall bear me also from the port.

EINAR.
Hurrah! My bridal-courser true ·
Think, Agnes, he is coming too!

BRAND.

But *I* am to a burial bound.

AGNES.

A burial.

EINAR.

You ?　Why, who is dead ?

BRAND.

The God who was your God, you said.

AGNES.

[*Shrinking back.*]

Come, Einar !

EINAR.

Brand !

BRAND.

　　　　　With cerements wound
The God of each mechanic slave,
Of each dull drudger, shall be laid
By broad day in his open grave.
End of the matter must be made ;
And high time is it you should know
He ail'd a thousand years ago.

EINAR.

Brand, you are ill !

BRAND.

　　　　　No, sound and fresh
As juniper and mountain-pine !
It is our age whose pining flesh
Craves burial at these hands of mine.
Ye will but laugh and love and play,
A little doctrine take on trust,
And all the bitter burden thrust

On One who came, ye have been told,
And from your shoulders took away
Your great transgressions manifold.
He bore for you the cross, the lance—
Ye therefore have full leave to dance ;
Dance then,—but where your dancing ends
Is quite another thing, my friends !

EINAR.

Ah, I perceive, the latest cry,
That folks are so much taken by.
You come of the new brood, who hold
That life is only gilded mould,
And with God's penal fires and flashes
Hound all the world to sack and ashes.

BRAND.

No, I am no " Evangelist,"
I speak not as the Church's priest ;
That I'm a Christian, even, I doubt ;
That I'm a man, though, I know well,
And that I see the cancer fell
That eats our country's marrow out.

EINAR.
[*Smiling.*]
I never heard, I must confess,
Our country taxed with being given
To worldly pleasure in excess !

BRAND.

No, by delight no breast is riven ;—
Were it but so, the ill were less !
Be passion's slave, be pleasure's thrall,—
But be it utterly, all in all !
Be not to-day, to-morrow, one,

Another when a year is gone;
Be what you are with all your heart,
And not by pieces and in part.
The Bacchant's clear, defined, complete,
The sot, his sordid counterfeit;
Silenus charms; but all his graces
The drunkard's parody debases.
Traverse the land from beach to beach,
Try every man in heart and soul,
You'll find he has no virtue whole,
But just a little grain of each.
A little pious in the pew,
A little grave,—his fathers' way,—
Over the cup a little gay,—
It was his father's fashion too!
A little warm when glasses clash,
And stormy cheer and song go round
For the small Folk, rock-will'd, rock-bound,
That never stood the scourge and lash.
A little free in promise-making;
And then, when vows in liquor will'd
Must be in mortal stress fulfill'd,
A little fine in promise-breaking.
Yet, as I say, all fragments still
His faults, his merits, fragments all,
Partial in good, partial in ill,
Partial in great things and in small;—
But here's the grief—that, worst or best,
Each fragment of him wrecks the rest!

EINAR.

Scoffing's an easy task: it were
A nobler policy to spare——

BRAND.

Perhaps, if it were wholesome too.

EINAR.

Well, well, the indictment I endorse
With all my heart; but can't divine
What in the world it has to do
With Him, the God you count a corse,
Whom yet I still acknowledge mine.

BRAND.

My genial friend, your gift is Art;—
Show me the God you have averr'd.
Him you have painted, I have heard,
And touch'd the honest people's heart.
Old is he haply; am I right?

EINAR.

Well, yes——

BRAND.

       Of course; and, doubtless, white?
Hairs straggling on a reverend head,
A beard of ice or silver-thread;
Kindly, yet stern enough to fright
A pack of children in the night.
I will not ask you, if your God
With fireside slippers you have shod;
But 'twere a pity, without doubt,
To leave skull-cap and glasses out.

EINAR.
[*Angrily.*]

What do you mean?

BRAND.

       I do not flout;
Just so he looks in form and face,

The household idol of our race.
As Catholics make of the Redeemer
A baby at the breast, so ye
Make God a dotard and a dreamer,
Verging on second infancy.
And as the Pope on Peter's throne
Calls little but his keys his own,
So to the Church you would confine
The world-wide realm of the Divine ;
'Twixt Life and Doctrine set a sea,
Nowise concern yourselves to be ;
Bliss for your souls ye would receive,
Not utterly and wholly live.
Ye need, such feebleness to brook,
A God who'll through his fingers look,
Who, like yourselves, is hoary grown,
And keeps a cap for his bald crown.
Mine is another kind of God !
Mine is a storm, where thine's a lull,
Implacable where thine's a clod,
All-loving there, where thine is dull ;
And He is young like Hercules,
No hoary sipper of life's lees !
His voice rang through the dazzled night
When He, within the burning wood,
By Moses upon Horeb's height
As by a pigmy's pigmy stood.
In Gibeon's vale He stay'd the sun,
And wonders without end has done,
And wonders without end would do,
Were not the age grown sick,—like you !

EINAR.

[Smiling faintly.]

And now the age shall be made whole ?

BRAND.

It shall, I say, and that as sure
As that I came to earth to cure
The sapping fester of its soul.

EINAR.

[*Shaking his head.*]

Ere yet the radiant torchlight blazes,
Throw not the taper to the ground!
Nor blot the antiquated phrases
Before the great new words be found!

BRAND.

Nothing that's new do I demand;
For Everlasting Right I stand.
It is not for a Church I cry,
It is not dogmas I defend;
Day dawn'd on both, and, possibly,
Day may on both of them descend.
What's made has " finis " for its brand;
Of moth and worm it feels the flaw,
And then, by nature and by law,
Is for an embryo thrust aside.
But there is one that shall abide ;—
The Spirit, that was never born,
That in the world's fresh gladsome Morn
Was rescued when it seem'd forlorn,
That built with valiant faith a road
Whereby from Flesh it climb'd to God.
Now but in shreds and scraps is dealt
The Spirit we have faintly felt ;
But from these scraps and from these shreds,
These headless hands and handless heads,
These torso-stumps of soul and thought,
A Man complete and whole shall grow,

And God His glorious child shall know,
His heir, the Adam that He wrought '

EINAR.

[*Breaking off.*]

Farewell.   I judge that it were best
We parted.

BRAND.

You are going west,
I northward.   To the fjord from here
Two pathways lead,—both alike near.
Farewell !

EINAR.

Farewell.

BRAND.

[*Turning round again.*]

Light learn to part
From vapour.—Know that Life's an art !

EINAR.

[*Waving him off.*]

Go, turn the universe upside down ;
Still in my ancient God I trust !

BRAND.

Good ; paint his crutches and his crown,—
I go to lay him in the dust !

[*Disappears over the pass.*

[EINAR *goes silently to the edge and looks after*
him.]

AGNES.

[*Stands a moment lost in thought ; then starts, looks*
about her uneasily, and asks :]

Is the sun set already ?

EINAR.
Nay,
A shadowing cloud; and now 'tis past.

AGNES.

The wind is cold !

EINAR.
Only a blast
That hurried by.   Here lies our way.

AGNES.

Yon mountain southward, sure, till now,
Wore not that black and beetling brow.

EINAR.

Thou saw'st it not for game and glee
Ere with his cry he startled thee.
Let him pursue his toilsome track,
And we will to our gambols back !

AGNES.

No, now I'm weary.

EINAR.
And indeed
I'm weary too, to tell the truth,—
And here our footing asks more heed
Than on yon upland broad and smooth.
But once we're on the level plain
We'll dance defiantly once more,
Ay, in a tenfold wilder vein
And tenfold swifter than before.
See Agnes, yon blue line that sparkles,
Fresh from the young sun's morning kiss,
And now it dimples and now darkles,
Silver one moment, amber this;

It is the ocean glad and free
That in the distance thou dost see.
And seest thou the smoky track
In endless line to leeward spread ?
And seest thou the point of black
Just rounding now the furthest head ?
It is the steamer—thine and mine—
And now it speeds into the fjord,
Then out into the foaming brine
To-night with thee and me on board !—
The mists have veil'd the mountain brow—
Saw'st thou how vividly, but now,
Heaven's image in the water woke!

AGNES.

[Looking absently about her.]
Oh, yes.   But tell me—sawest thou——?

EINAR.

What ?

AGNES.

[In a hushed voice, without looking at him.]
How he tower'd as he spoke ?
   [She goes down over the pass, EINAR follows.

[A path along the crags, with a wild valley beyond to
  the right.   Above, and beyond the mountain,
  are glimpses of greater heights, with peaks and
  snow.]

BRAND.

[Comes up along the path, descends, stops half-way
  upon a jutting crag, and gazes into the valley.]
Yes, I know myself once more !
Every boat-house by the shore,

Every home; the landslip-fall,
And the inlet's fringe of birch,
And the ancient moulder'd church,
And the river alders, all
From my boyhood I recall.
But methinks it all has grown
Grayer, smaller than I knew;
Yon snow-cornice hangs more prone
Than of old it used to do,
From that scanty heaven encloses
Yet another strip of blue,
Beetles, looms, immures, imposes—
Steals of light a larger due.
  [*Sits down and gazes into the distance.*]
And the fjord too. Crouch'd it then
In so drear and deep a den?
'Tis a squall. A square-rigg'd skiff
Scuds before it to the land.
Southward, shadow'd by the cliff,
I descry a wharf, a shed,
Then, a farm-house, painted red.—
'Tis the farm beside the strand!
'Tis the widow's farm. The home
Of my childhood. Thronging come
Memories born of memories dead.
I, where yonder breakers roll,
Grew, a lonely infant-soul.
 Like a nightmare on my heart
Weighs the burden of my birth,
Knit to one, who walks apart
With her spirit set to earth.
All the high emprise that stirr'd
In me, now is veil'd and blurr'd.
Force and valour from me fail,
Heart and soul grow faint and frail
As I near my home, I change,

To my very self grow strange—
Wake, as baffled Samson woke,
Shorn and fetter'd, tamed and broke.
　　　[Looks again down into the valley.]
What is stirring down below ?
Out of every garth they flow,
Troops of children, wives and men,
And in long lines meet and mingle,
Now among the rocks and shingle
Vanish, now emerge again ;—
To the ancient Church they go.
　　　　　[Rises.]
Oh, I know you, through and through !
Sluggard spirits, souls of lead !
All the Lord's Prayer, said by you,
Is not with such anguish sped,
By such passion borne on high,
That one tittle thrills the sky
As a ringing human cry,
Save the prayer for daily bread !
That's this people's battle-call,
That's the blazon of them all !
From its context pluck'd apart,
Branded deep in every heart—
There it lies, the tempest-tost
Wreckage of the Faith you've lost.
Forth ! out of this stifling pit !
Vault-like is the air of it !
Not a Flag may float unfurl'd
In this dead and windless world !
　　　[He is going ; a stone is thrown from
　　　　above and rolls down the slope close by
　　　　him.
　　　　　BRAND.
　　　　[Calling upward.]
Ha ! who throws stones there ?

GERD.

[*A girl of fifteen, running along the crest with
stones in her apron.*]

Ho!   Good aim!

He screams!

[*She throws again.*]

BRAND.

Hullo, child, stop that game!

GERD.

Without a hurt he's sitting now,
And swinging on a wind-swept bough!

[*She throws again and screams.*]

Now fierce as ever he's making for me.
Help!   Hoo!   With claws he'll rend and gore
 me!

BRAND.

In the Lord's name——

GERD.

Whist! who are you?

Hold still. hold still ; he's flying.

BRAND.

Who ?

GERD.

Didn't you see the falcon fly ?

BRAND.

Here ? no.

GERD.

The laidly fowl with crest
Thwart on its sloping brow depress'd,
And red-and-yellow circled eye

BRAND.

Which is your way ?

GERD.

To church I go.

BRAND.

Then we can go along together.

GERD.
[*Pointing upward.*]
We ?   But the way I'm bound is thither.

BRAND.
[*Pointing downward.*]
But yonder is the church, you know !

GERD.
[*Pointing downward with a scornful smile.*]
That yonder ?

BRAND.

Truly ; come with me.

GERD.

No ; yon is ugly.

BRAND.

Ugly ?   Why ?

GERD.

Because it's small.

BRAND.

Where did you see

A greater ?

GERD.

I could tell you, I.

Farewell.   [*She turns away upwards.*

III   C

BRAND.

      Lies there that church of yours ?
Why, that way leads but to the moors.

GERD.

Come with me, you ; I've got to show
A church that's built of ice and snow !

BRAND.

Of ice and snow !   I see the truth !
There, amid peak and precipice
As I remember from my youth,
There yawns a cavernous abyss ;
" Ice-church " they call'd the place of old ;
And of it many a tale was told ;
A frozen tarn has paved the floor ;
Aloft, in massy-piled blocks,
The gather'd snow-drifts slope and soar
Arch-like over the yawning rocks.

GERD.

It seems a mountain-cleft,—ah, yes,
It is a church, though, none the less.

BRAND.

Never go there ; a sudden gust
Has often crack'd that hollow crust ;
A rifle shot, a scream, a whoop——

GERD.

[Without listening to him.]
Just come and see a reindeer troop
Gulf'd in the fall, and never found
Till spring and the great thaw came round.

BRAND.

Yonder is danger ; go not near it !

GERD.
[*Pointing down.*]
Yonder is foulness ; thou must fear it !

BRAND.

God's peace with you !

GERD.
　　　　　　　　Nay, this way pass !
Yonder the cataract's singing Mass ;
There on the crags the whistling weather
Preaches you hot and cold together.
Thither the hawk will ne'er steal in ;
Down, down he sweeps from Svartetind,—
Yonder he sits, the ugly block,
Like my church-steeple's weathercock.

BRAND.

Wild is thy way, and wild thy soul,—
A cittern with a shatter'd bowl.
Of dulness dulness is the brood,—
But evil's lightly won to good.

GERD.

With whirring wings I hear him come !
I'll e'en make shift to get me home !
In yonder church I'm safe,—farewell ;
He's on me,—hoo, how fierce and fell !
　　　　　　[*She screams.*]
I'll throw a stone !　No nearer, now .
If thou hast talons, I've a bough !
　　　　　　[*She runs off up the mountain.*

BRAND.

[After a pause.]

This was a church-goer, like the rest.
Mountain- or Dale-church, which is best?
Which wildest reel, which blindest grope,
Which furthest roam from home and hope:—
Light-heart who, crown'd with leafage gay,
Loves by the dizziest verge to play,—
Faint-heart, who marches slack and slow,
Because old Wont will have it so;—
Wild-heart, who, borne on lawless wings,
Sees fairness in the foulest things?
War front and rear, war high and low,
With this fell triple-banded foe!
I see my Call! It gleams ahead
Like sunshine through a loop-hole shed!
I know my task; these demons slain,
The sick Earth shall grow sound again;—
Once let them to the grave be given,
The fever-fumes of Earth shall fly!
Up, Soul, array thee! Sword from thigh!
To battle for the heirs of Heaven!

[He descends to the hamlet.

ACT SECOND

By the fjord-side, steep precipices all around. The ancient and tumble-down church stands on a little knoll hard by. A storm is coming on.

The country-folk,—men, women, and children,—are gathered in knots, some on the shore, some on the slopes. The MAYOR *sits in the midst, on a stone; a* CLERK *is helping him; corn and provisions are being distributed.* EINAR *and* AGNES *stand surrounded by a crowd, a little apart. Some boats lie on the beach.* BRAND *comes forward, unnoticed to the church-knoll.*

A MAN.
[*Breaking through the crowd.*]
Out of the way '

A WOMAN.
I'm first !

THE MAN.
[*Thrusting her aside.*]
Get back !
[*Pushing towards the* MAYOR.]
Ho ! look you, fill me up my sack !

THE MAYOR.
All in good time.

THE MAN.

I cannot stay ;—
I've four—five—babes of bread bereft !

THE MAYOR.
[*Facetiously.*]
You don't know just how many, en

THE MAN.
One was e'en dying when I left.

THE MAYOR.
Hold.   You are enter'd, are you not ?
[*Examines his papers.*]
No.   Yes, you are though.   Well for you.
[*To the* CLERK.]
Give Number Twenty-nine his lot.
Come, come, good folks, be patient, do !
Nils Snemyr ?

A MAN.
Ay, ay !

THE MAYOR.
We must pare
A quarter off your former share.
You're fewer now, you know.

THE MAN.
Yes, yes,—
My Ragnhild died yestreen.

THE MAYOR.
[*Making a note.*]
One less.
Saving is saving, howsoe'er.
[*To the* MAN, *who is retiring.*]

But look you, now, you needn't run
And marry another on the spot !

CLERK.
[*Sniggering.*]

Hee, hee !

THE MAYOR.
[*Sharply.*]
You laugh ?

CLERK.
Your Worship's fun
Is irresistible.

THE MAYOR.
Have done !
This work's no jesting ; but the best
Method with mourners is a jest.

EINAR.
[*Coming out of the throng with* AGNES.]
Now my last pocket's clean and bare,
Spent every stiver, every note ;—
A very beggar I go afloat,
And pawn my watch to pay my fare !

THE MAYOR.
Yes, in good time you came along.
What I've collected is a song,—
By no means answers to the call
When needy hand and mouth ill-fed
Must halve the sharing of shared bread
With those who've ne'er a bit at all.
[*He perceives* BRAND, *and points up to him.*]
One more !   You're welcome !   If report

Of our drought-flood-and-famine curse
Has reach'd you, promptly loose your purse
(If yet unloosen'd).　Every sort
Of contribution meets the case.
Our store's nigh spent.　Five fishes scant
In the wide wilderness of Want
Don't make a square meal nowadays.

BRAND.

Myriads, idolatrously given,
Would lift the soul no nearer heaven.

THE MAYOR.

It was not words I bade you share :
They're barren when the belly's bare.

EINAR.

I can't believe that you recall
What long and fierce calamities
They've suffered :—famine, drought, disease.
Men die, Brand——

BRAND.

　　　　　　I perceive it all.
Each livid-circled eye makes clear
Who it is holds assizes here.

THE MAYOR.

Yet there you stand, a very flint !

BRAND.

If life here ran its sluggish round
Of common toil and common stint,
Pity with me your pangs had found.
Who homeward crawls with earth-set eyes,
In him the sleeping beast will rise.

When days in drowsy calm go by,
Like funerals, at walking pace,
You well may fear that the Most High
Has struck you from His Book of Grace.
But unto you He was more good,
He scatter'd terror in your blood,
He scourged you with the rods that slay,
The gifts He gave, He took away——

VOICES.
[*Fiercely interrupting him.*]
He mocks us in our bitter need !

THE MAYOR.
He rails at us who tend and feed !

BRAND.
[*Shaking his head.*]
Oh, if the blood of all my heart
Could heal you from the hunger-smart,
In welling streams it should be shed,
Till every vein was a dry bed.
But here it were a sin to give !
God seeks to pluck you from your bane ;—
Nations, though poor and sparse, that live,
Suck might and marrow from their pain.
The purblind sight takes falcon-wing,
Sees clear into the heart of things,
The faltering will stands stout at bay,
And sees the triumph through the fray.
But men whom misery has not mann'd
Are worthless of the saving hand !

A WOMAN.
Yonder a storm breaks on the fjord,
As if awaken'd by his word !

ANOTHER WOMAN.

He tempts God ! Mark what I foretell .

BRAND.

Your God ne'er wrought a miracle !

WOMEN.

See, see ! the storm '

VOICES AMONG THE THRONG.

Stab,—stone him ! chase
The flinty fellow from the place !

[*The peasants close menacingly round* BRAND. *The*
MAYOR *intervenes.* A WOMAN, *wild and dis-
hevelled, comes hurriedly down the slopes.*]

THE WOMAN.
[*Crying out towards the throng.*]
Oh, where is help, for Jesus' grace '

THE MAYOR.

What do you need ? Explain your case.

THE WOMAN.

Nothing I need ; no alms I seek,
But oh, the horror, horror——

THE MAYOR.

Speak !

THE WOMAN.

I have no voice,—O comfort, aid !
Where is the priest ?

THE MAYOR.

Here there is none—

THE WOMAN.

I am undone !   I am undone !
Stern wast thou, God, when I was made !

BRAND.
[*Approaching.*]
Maybe, however, there is one.

THE WOMAN.
[*Seizing his arm.*]
Then let him come, and swiftly !

BRAND.
                                        Tell
Your need, and he will surely come.

THE WOMAN.
Across the fjord—my husband———

BRAND.
                                        Well ?

THE WOMAN.
Three starving babes, and ne'er a crumb,———
Say no,—he is not sent to hell !

BRAND.
Your story first.

THE WOMAN.
              My breast was dry ;
Man sent no help, and God was dumb ;
My babe was dying in agony ;
Cut to the heart,—his child he slew !—

BRAND.
He slew——— !

THE THRONG.
[*Shuddering.*]
His child :

THE WOMAN.

                        At once he knew
The horror of his deed of blood !
His grief ran brimming like a flood ;
He struck himself the death-wound too.
Come, save him, save him from perdition,
Spite of wild water and wild sky !
He cannot live, and dare not die !
There lies he, clasping the dead frame,
And shrieking on the Devil's name \

BRAND.
[*Quietly.*]
Yes, here is need.

EINAR.
[*Pale.*]
          Great God on high

THE MAYOR.
He doesn't live in my Division.

BRAND.
[*Curtly, to the Peasants.*]
Unmoor a boat and row me there !

A MAN.
When such a storm is up ?   Who dare ?

THE MAYOR.
A path goes round the fjord——

THE WOMAN.

Nay, nay,

There's now no practicable way;
The footbridge as I came across
Was broken by the foaming foss.

BRAND.

Unmoor the boat.

A MAN.

It can't be done;

O'er rock and reef the breakers run.

ANOTHER.

Down sweeps a blast!   See, at a stroke
The whole fjord vanishes in smoke!

A THIRD.

With waves so wild and wind so rough,
The Dean would put the service off.

BRAND.

A sinful soul that nears its end
Waits not until the weather mend!
    [*Goes down to a boat and looses the sail.*]
You'll risk the boat?

THE OWNER.

I will; but stay!

BRAND.

Now, who will risk his life, I say?

A MAN.

I'll not go with him.

ANOTHER.
No, nor I.

SEVERAL.
It were just putting out to die!

BRAND.
Your God helps none across the fjord;
Remember, though, that mine's on board!

THE WOMAN.
[*Wringing her hands.*]
He'll die unsaved!

BRAND.
[*Calling from the boat.*]
                    One will avail
To bail the leakage, shift the sail;
Come, one of you that lately gave;
Give now to death and to the grave

SEVERAL.
[*Shrinking back.*]
Never ask such-like of us!

ONE.
[*Menacingly.*]
                    Land!
'Tis overbold to tempt God's hand!

SEVERAL VOICES.
See, the storm thickens!

OTHERS.
                    The ropes break!

BRAND.
[*Holding himself fast with the boat-hook, and calling
to the strange* WOMAN.]
Good ; come then you ; but speedily !

THE WOMAN.
[*Shrinking back.*]
I ! Where no others———— !

BRAND.
Let them be !

THE WOMAN.
I cannot !

BRAND.
Cannot ?

THE WOMAN.
My babes' sake———— !

BRAND.
[*Scornfully laughing.*]
You build upon a quaking sand !

AGNES.
[*Turns with glowing cheeks to* EINAR, *lays her hand
on his arm, and says :*]
Did you hear all ?

EINAR.
A valiant heart.

AGNES.
Thank God, Einar, you see your part
[*Calls to* BRAND.]

See,—here is one man, brave and true,
To go the saving way with you !

BRAND.

Come on then !

EINAR.

[*Pale.*]

    I !

AGNES.

        I give you !   Go !
Mine eyes are lifted, that were low '

EINAR.

Ere I found you, with willing feet
I would have follow'd where he led——

AGNES.

[*Trembling.*]

But now—— !

EINAR.

My life is new and sweet ;—

I cannot go !

AGNES.

[*Starting back.*]

What have you said !

EINAR.

I dare not go !

AGNES.

[*With a cry.*]

Now roars a sea

Of sweeping flood and surging foam
World-wide, world-deep, 'twixt you and me !
[*To* BRAND.]
I will go with you !

BRAND.

Good ; then come !

EINAR.

[*Clutching desperately after her.*]

Agnes !

THE WHOLE THRONG.

[*Hurrying towards her.*]

Come back ! Come back !

WOMEN.

[*In terror as she springs into the boat.*]

Help, Lord !

BRAND.

Where does the house lie !

WOMEN.

[*Pointing*].

By the fjord,

Behind yon black and jutting brink !

[*The boats put out.*

EINAR.

[*Calling after them.*]

Your home, your mother, Agnes ! Think !
O save yourself !

AGNES.

We are three on board !

[*The boat sails. The people crowd together
on the slopes, and watch in eager sus-
pense.*

A MAN.

He clears the headland !

ANOTHER.

Nay !

III   D

THE FIRST.

                 Yes, see,—
Astern he has it, and in lee!

ANOTHER.
A squall! It's caught them!

THE MAYOR.

              Look at that,—
The wind has swept away his hat!

A WOMAN.
Black as a rook's wing, his wet hair
Streams backward on the angry air.

FIRST MAN.
All seethes and surges!

EINAR.

            What a yell!
Rang through the storm!

A WOMAN.

              'Twas from the fell.

ANOTHER.
[*Pointing up.*]
See, there stands Gerd upon the cliff,
Hallooing at the passing skiff!

FIRST WOMAN.
She's flinging pebbles like witch-corn,
And blowing through a twisted horn.

SECOND WOMAN.
Now she has slung it like a wand,
And pipes upon her hollow'd hand.

A MAN.

Ay, pipe away, thou troll abhorr'd !
He has a Guide and Guard on board !

ANOTHER.

In a worse storm, with him to steer,
I'd put to sea and never fear.

FIRST MAN.
[To EINAR.]

What is he ?

EINAR.

A priest.

SECOND MAN.

Wnat is he, nay—
That's plain : he is a man, I say !
Strong will is in him, and bold deed.

FIRST MAN.

That were the very priest we need !

MANY VOICES.

Ay, ay, the very priest we need !

[They disperse along the slopes.

THE MAYOR.
[Collecting his books and papers.]

Well, 'tis opposed to all routine
To labour in a strange vocation,
Intrusively to risk one's skin
Without an adequate occasion.—
I do my duty with precision,—
But always in my own Division.   [Goes.

[Outside the hut on the Ness. Late afternoon. The
   fjord is smooth and gleaming. AGNES is sitting

by the beach.   Presently BRAND *comes out of
the hut.*]

BRAND.

That was death.   The horror-rifted
Bosom at its touch grew whole.
Now he looks a calm great soul,
All illumined and up-lifted.
Has a false illusion might
Out of gloom to win such light ?
    Of his devil's-deed he saw
Nothing but the outward flaw,—
That of it which tongue can tell
And to hands is palpable,—
That for which his name's reviled,—
The brute slaying of his child.
    But those two, that sat and gazed
With great frighten'd eyes, amazed,
Speechless, like two closely couching
Birdlets, in the ingle crouching,—
Who but look'd, and look'd, and ever
Look'd, unwitting upon what,—
In whose souls a poison-spot
Bit and sank, which they shall never
Even as old men bent and gray,
In Time's turmoil wear away,—
They, whose tide of life proceeds
From this fountain of affright,
Who by dark and dreadful deeds
Must be nurtured into light,
Nor by any purging flames
May that carrion thought consume,—
This he saw not, being blind,
That the direst of the doom
Was the doom he left behind.
    And from them shall haply rise
Link'd offences one by one.

Wherefore ?   The abyss replies :
From the father sprang the son !
What shall be by Love erased ?
What be quietly effaced ?
Where, O where, does guilt begin
In our heritage of sin ?
What Assizes, what Assessors,
When that Judgment is declared ?
Who shall question, who be heard,
Where we're all alike transgressors ?
Who will venture then to plead
His foul-borrow'd title-deed ?
Will the old answer profit yet :
" From my father dates my debt ? "
O, abysmal as the night,
Riddle, who can read thee right !
But the people dance light-footed,
Heedless by the dizzy brink ;
Where the soul should cry and shrink,
None has vision to perceive
What uptowering guilt is rooted
In that little word : We live.

[*Some men of the community come from behind the
house and approach* BRAND.]

A MAN.

We were to meet again, you see.

BRAND.

His need of human help has ceased.

THE MAN.

Yes ; he is ransom'd and released ;
But in the chamber still sit three.

BRAND.

And what then ?

THE MAN.

Of the scraps we got
Together, a few crumbs we've brought——

BRAND.

Though you give all, and life retain,
I tell you that your gift is vain.

THE MAN.

Had he to-day, who now lies dead,
By mortal peril been bested,
And I had heard his foundering cry,
I also would have dared to die.

BRAND.

But peril of the Soul you slight?

THE MAN.

Well, we're but drudgers day by day.

BRAND.

Then from the downward-streaming light
Turn your eyes utterly away;
And cease to cast the left askance
At heaven, while with the right you glance
Down at the mould where, crouching low,
Self-harness'd in the yoke you go.

THE MAN.

I thought you'd say we ought to shake us
Free of the yoke we toil in?

BRAND.
                              Yea,
If you are able.

THE MAN.
You can make us!

BRAND.
Can I?

THE MAN.
Full many have been sent
Who told us truly of the way;
The path they pointed to, you went.

BRAND.
You mean——— ?

THE MAN.
A thousand speeches Brand
Less deeply than one dint of deed.
Here in our fellows' name we stand;—
We see, a man is what we need.

BRAND.
[*Uneasily.*]
What will you with me?

THE MAN.
Be our priest.

BRAND.
I? Here!

THE MAN.
You've maybe heard it told,
There is no pastor for this fold.

BRAND.
Yes; I recall.

THE MAN.
The place of old
Was large, which now is of the least.

When evil seasons froze the field,
And blight on herdsman fell,
When want struck down the Man, and seal'd
The Spirit with its drowsing spell,
When there was dearth of beef and brew,—
Then came a dearth of parsons too.

BRAND.

Aught else : but this ye must not ask !
I'm summoned to a greater task.
The great world's open ear I seek ;
Through Life's vast organ I must speak.
What should I here ?   By mountains pent
The voice of man falls impotent.

THE MAN.

By mountains echoed, longer heard
Is each reverberating word.

BRAND.

Who in a cavern would be bound,
When broad meads beckon all around ?
Who'll sweat to plough the barren land
When there are fruitful fields at hand ?
Who'll rear his fruitage from the seed
When orchards ripen to the skies ?
Who'll struggle on with daily need
When vision gives him wings and eyes ?

THE MAN.
[*Shaking his head.*]
Your deed I fathom'd,—not your word.

BRAND.
[*Going.*]
Question no more !   On board ! on board !

THE MAN.
[*Barring his way.*]
This calling that you must fulfil,
This work, whereon you've set your will,
Is it so precious to you, say ?

BRAND.
It is my very life !

THE MAN.
                Then stay !
                [*Pointedly.*]
" Though you give all and life retain,
Remember, that your gift is vain."

BRAND.
One thing is yours you may not spend ?
Your very inmost Self of all.
You may not bind it, may not bend,
Nor stem the river of your call.
To make for ocean is its end.

THE MAN.
Though tarn and moorland held it fast,—
As dew 'twould reach the sea at last.

BRAND.
[*Looking fixedly at him.*]
Who gave you power to answer thus ?

THE MAN.
You, by your deed, you gave it us.
When wind and water raged and roar'd,
And you launch'd out through wind and wave,
When, a poor sinning soul to save,
You set your life upon a board,

Deep into many a heart it fell,
Like wind and sunshine, cold and hot,
Rang through them like a chiming bell,—
       [*With lowered voice.*]
To-morrow, haply, all's forgot,
And furl'd the kindling banner bright
You just now lifted in our sight.

BRAND.

Duty is not, where power is not.
       [*Sternly.*]
If you cannot be what you ought,
Be in good earnest what you may;
Be heart and soul a man of clay.

THE MAN.

      [*After gazing on him a moment.*]
Woe! you, who quench the lamp you lit;
And us, who had a glimpse of it!
      [*He goes ; the others silently follow.*]

BRAND.

      [*After long watching them.*]
Homewards, one by one, with flagging
Spirits, heavily and slow,
Foreheads bowed, and weary lagging
Footsteps, silently they go.
Each with sorrow in his eyes,
Walks as from a lifted rod,
Walks like Adam spurn'd by God
From the gates of Paradise,—
Walks like him, with sin-veil'd sight,—
Sees, like him, the gathering night,
All his gain of knowledge shares,
All his loss of blindness bears.

I have boldly dared to plan
The refashioning of Man,—
—There's my work,—Sin's image grown,
Whom God moulded in His own.—
Forth ! to wider fields away !
Here's no room for battle-play !
    [*Going ; but pauses as he sees* AGNES *by*
              the beach.]
See, she listens by the shore,
As to airy songs afloat.
So she listen'd in the boat
As the stormy surge it tore,—
Listening, to the thwart she clung,—
Listening still, the sea-foam hoar
From her open forehead flung.
'Tis as though her ear were changing
Function, and her eye were listening.
             [*He approaches.*]
Maiden, is it o'er those glistening
Reaches that your eye is ranging ?

            AGNES.
     [*Without turning round.*]
Neither those nor aught of earth ;
Nothing of them I descry.
But a greater earth there gleams
Sharply outlined on the sky,
Foaming floods and spreading streams,
Mists and sunshine breaking forth.
Scarlet-shafted flames are playing
Over cloud-capp'd mountain heads,
And an endless desert spreads,
Whereupon great palms are swaying
In the bitter-breathing blast.
Swart the shadows that they cast.
Nowhere any living thing ;

Like a new world at its birth ;
And I hear strange accents ring,
And a Voice interpreting :
" Choose thy endless loss or gain,
Do thy work and bear thy pain ;—
Thou shalt people this new earth ! "

BRAND.
[*Carried away.*]
Say, what further !

AGNES.
[*Laying her hand on her breast.*]
                        In my soul
I can feel new powers awaking,
I can see a dayspring breaking,
I can feel full floods that roll,
And my heart grows larger, freer,
Clasps the world within its girth,
And a voice interprets : Here
Shalt thou people a new earth !
All the thoughts that men shall utter,
All the deeds men shall achieve,
Waken, whisper, quiver, mutter,
As if now they were to live ;
And I rather feel than see
Him who sits enthroned above,
Feel that He looks down on me
Full of sadness and of love,
Tender-bright as morning's breath,
And yet sorrowing unto death :
And I hear strange accents wake :
" Now thou must be made, and make ;
Choose thy endless loss or gain !—
Do thy work and bear thy pain ! "

BRAND.

Inwards!　In!　O word of might,
Now I see my way aright.
In ourselves is that young Earth,
Ripe for the divine new-birth;
Will, the fiend, must there be slain,
Adam there be born again.
Let the world then take its way,
Brutal toil or giddy play;
But if e'er we meet in fight,
If my work it seek to blight,
Then, by heaven, I'll smite and slay!
Room within the wide world's span,
Self completely to fulfil,—
That's a valid right of Man,
And no more than that I will!
　　　　[*After pondering awhile in silence.*]
To fulfil oneself!　And yet,
With a heritage of debt?
　　　　　　[*Pauses and looks out.*]
Who is she, that, stooping deep,
Chambers hither up the steep,—
Crooked back and craning crop?
Now for breath she has to stop,
Clutches wildly lest she stumble,
And her skinny fingers fumble
Fierce for something that she drags
In those deep and roomy bags.
Skirt, like folds of feather'd skin,
Dangling down her shrivelled shin;
Hands, a pair of clenched hooks;
So the eagle's carcase looks
Nail'd against the barn-door top.
　　　　　　[*In sudden anguish.*]
What chill memories upstart,—
O what gusts from childhood dart

Frosty showers on her—and other
Fiercer frost upon my heart— ?
God of grace ! It is my Mother !

BRAND'S MOTHER.

[*Comes up, stops when half seen above the slope,
    holds her hand up to shade her eyes, and looks
    round.*]
He's here, they told me.
                [*Coming nearer.*]
                        Drat the blaze,—
It nearly takes away my sight !
Son, is that you ?

BRAND.
            Yes.

HIS MOTHER.
[*Rubbing her eyes.*]
                    Hoo, those rays,
They burn one's very eyes outright ;
I can't tell priest from boor.

BRAND.
                        Sun's light
At home I never saw at all
'Twixt fall of leaf and cuckoo's call.

HIS MOTHER.
[*Laughing quietly.*]
Ay, there 'tis good. One's gripped with frost
Like icicles o'er a plunging river,
Strong to dare anything whatever,
—And yet believe one is not lost.

BRAND.
Farewell. My leisure time is spent.

HIS MOTHER.

Ay, thou wast ever loth to stay.
As boy thou long'dst to be away—

BRAND.

It was at your desire I went.

HIS MOTHER.

Ay, and good reason too, I say
'Twas needful thou shouldst be a priest.
　　[Examines him more closely.]
H'm, he is grown up strong and tall.
But heed this word of mine, at least,—
Care for thy life, son !

BRAND.

　　　　　　Is that all ?

HIS MOTHER.

Thy life ?　What's dearer ?

BRAND.

　　　　　　　　I would say:
Have you more counsels to convey ?

HIS MOTHER.

For others, use them as you may,
And welcome.　But thy life, O save it
For my sake ; it was I that gave it.
　　[Angrily.]
Your mad deed's talked of far and near ;
It scares and harrows me to hear.
On such a day to dare the fjord,
And squander what you're bound to hoard '
You of our clan survive alone,
You are my son, my flesh and bone ;

The roof-tree beam that copes and clinches
The house I've builded up by inches.
Stick fast; hold out; endure; survive!
Guard your life! Never let it go!
An heir is bound to keep alive,—
And you'll be mine—one day—you know——

BRAND.

Indeed? And that was why you plann'd
With loaded purse to seek me here?

His MOTHER.

Son, are you raving?
                [*Steps back.*]
                        Don't come near
Stay where you are! You'll feel my hand!
                [*More calmly.*]
What were you meaning?—Just attend
I'm getting older year by year;
Sooner or later comes the end;
Then you'll inherit all I've treasured,
'Tis duly counted, weighed and measured—
Nay, nay, I've nothing on me now!—
It's all at home. It is but scant;
But he that gets it will not want.
Stand back there! Don't come near!—I vow
I'll fling no stiver of my store
Down fissures, nor in spot unknown
Hide any, nor below a stone.
In wall, or underneath a floor;
All shall be yours, son, you shall be
My sole and single legatee.

BRAND.

And the conditions ?

HIS MOTHER.

One I make,

No more ; don't set your life at stake.
Keep up our family and name,
That's all the gratitude I claim.
Then see that nothing go to waste,—
Naught be divided or displaced ;—
Add much or little, as you will ;
But O preserve, preserve it still !

BRAND.

[After a short pause.]

One thing needs clearing 'twixt us two.
From childhood I have thwarted you ;—
You've been no mother, I no son,
Till you are gray, my childhood gone.

HIS MOTHER.

I do not ask to be caress'd.
Be what you please ; I am not nice.
Be stern, be fierce, be cold as ice,
It will not cleave my armour'd breast ;
Keep, though you hoard it, what was mine,
And never let it leave our line !

BRAND.

[Going a step nearer.]

And if I took it in my head
To strew it to the winds, instead ?

HIS MOTHER.
[Reeling back.]

Strew, what through all these years of care
Has bent my back and bleach'd my hair ?

III   E

BRAND.

[Nodding slowly.]

To strew it.

HIS MOTHER.

Strew it !   If you do,
It is my soul that you will strew !

BRAND.

And if I do it, even so ?
If I one evening vigil keep
With lighted taper by your bed,
While you with clasped Psalter sleep
The first night's slumber of the dead,—
If I then fumble round about,
Draw treasure after treasure out,
Take up the taper, hold it low— ?

HIS MOTHER.

[Approaching excitedly.]

Whence comes this fancy ?

BRAND.

Would you know ?

HIS MOTHER.

Ay.

BRAND.

From a childish scene that still
Lives in my mind, and ever will,
That seams my soul with foul device
Like an infestering cicatrice.
It was an autumn evening.   Dead
Was father ; you lay sick in bed.
I stole where he was laid by night,
All pallid in the silver light.

I stood and watched him from my nook,
Saw how his two hands clasp'd the Book;
I marvell'd why he slept so long,
Mark'd his thin wrists, and smelt the strong
Odour of linen newly dried;——
And then I heard a step outside;——
A woman enter'd, strode apace
Up to the bed, nor saw my face.
Then she began to grope and pry;
First put the corpse's vesture by,
Drew forth a bundle, then a store,
Counted, and whisper'd : There is more !
Then, grubbing deeper in the ground,
Clutch'd a seal'd packet tightly bound,
With trembling fingers strove and tore,
Bit it in two, groped deeper, found,
Counted, and whisper'd : There is more !
She cried, she cursed, she wail'd, she wept,
She scented where the treasure lay,
And then with eager anguish swept
Down like a falcon on her prey.
When she had ransacked all the room,
She turn'd, like one who hears her doom,
Wrapp'd up her booty in a shawl,
And faintly groan'd : So that was all !

His Mother.

I needed much, I little won ;
And very dearly was it bought.

Brand.

Even more dearly than you thought ;
Son's-heart you shatter'd in your son.

His Mother.

Tut, tut.　To barter hearts for gold

Was customary from of old.
Still dearer once I had to pay,—
I think I gave my life away.
Something I gave that now is not ;—
I seem to see it flash in air
Like something foolish and yet fair ;
I gave—I know not rightly what ;—
" Love " was the name it used to bear.—
I know it was a bitter choice ;
I know my father gave his voice :
" Forget the peasant-boy and wed
The other, 'spite his frosty pate ;
A fellow with a knowing head,
He'll fairly double the estate ! "
I took him, and he brought me shame.
The doubled gettings never came.
But I have drudged with streaming brow,
And there is little lacking now.

BRAND.

And do you, as you near your grave,
Know that it was your soul you gave ?

HIS MOTHER.

It's clear that I knew that, at least,
Giving my son to be a priest.
When the hour comes, a grateful heir
Of my salvation will take care ;
I own the acres and the pence,
And you the deathbed eloquence.

BRAND.

With all your cunning you mistook ;
You read me wrong in childhood's book.
And many dwell by bank and brae
Who love their children in that way ;—

A child's a steward, you suppose,
Of the parental cast-off clothes ;
A glimpse of the Eternal flits
At times across your wandering wits ;
You snatch at it, and dream you spring
Into the essence of the thing
By grafting Riches upon Race ;—
That Death with Life you can displace,
That years, if steadily amass'd,
Will yield Eternity at last.

His Mother.

Don't rummage in your Mother's mind,
But take what she will leave behind.

Brand.

The debt as well ?

His Mother.

　　　　　The debt ?　What debt ?
There is none.

Brand.

　　　　　Very good ; but yet
Suppose there were,—I should be bound
To settle every claim I found.
The son must satisfy each call
Before the mother's burial.
Though but four empty walls I took,
I still should own your debit-book.

His Mother.

No law commands it.

Brand.

　　　　　　Not the kind
That ink on parchment ever writ ;
But deep in every honest mind

Another law is burnt and bit,—
And that I execute.   Thou blind !
Learn to have sight !   Thou hast debased
The dwelling-place of God on earth,
The spirit He lent thee hast laid waste,
The image that thou bor'st at birth
With mould and filthiness defaced ;
Thy Soul, that once had flight and song,
Thrust, clipp'd, among the common throng.
That is your debt.   What will you do
When God demands His own of you ?

HIS MOTHER.
[*Confused.*]
What will I do ?   Do ?——

BRAND.
Never fear ;
I take your debt upon me whole.
God's image, blotted in your soul,
In mine, Will-cleansed, shall stand clear.
Go with good courage to your rest.
By debt you shall not sleep oppress'd.

HIS MOTHER.
My debt and sin you'll wipe away ?

BRAND.
Your debt.   Observe.   The debt : no more.
Your debt alone I can repay ;
Your sin yourself must answer for.
The sum of native human worth
Crush'd in the brutish toil of earth
Can verily by human aid
To the last atom be repaid ;
But in the losing of it lies
The sin, which who repents not—dies !

HIS MOTHER.
[*Uneasily.*]
Twere best I took my homeward way
To the deep valley, to the gloom ;
Such rank and poisonous fancies bloom
In this insufferable ray ;
I'm almost fainting at the fume.

BRAND.
Seek you the shadow ; I abide.
And if you long for light and sky,
And fain would see me ere you die,
Call me, and I am by your side.

HIS MOTHER.
Yes, with a sermon on my doom !

BRAND.
No, tender both as priest and child
I'll shield you from the wind of dread,
And singing low beside your bed
Lull to repose your anguish wild.

HIS MOTHER.
And that with lifted hand you swear?

BRAND.
When you repent I will be there.
[*Approaching her.*]
But I too make conditions. Hear.
Whatever in this world is dear
Willingly you must from you rend,
And naked to the grave descend.

HIS MOTHER.
[*Wildly repulsing him.*]
Bid fire be sever'd from its heat,

Snow from its cold, wave from its wet !
Ask less !

BRAND.

Toss a babe overboard,
And beg the blessing of the Lord.

HIS MOTHER.

Ask something else : ask hunger, thirst,—
But not what all men deem the worst !

BRAND.

If just that worst is asked in vain,
No other can His grace obtain.

HIS MOTHER.

A money-alms I will present you !

BRAND.

All ?

HIS MOTHER.

All ! Son, will not much content you ?

BRAND.

Your guilt you never shall put by
Till you, like Job, in ashes die.

HIS MOTHER.
[*Wringing her hands.*]

My life destroy'd, my soul denied,
My goods soon scatter'd far and wide !
Home then, and in these fond arms twine
All that I still can say is mine !
My treasure, child in anguish born,
For thee my bleeding breast was torn ;—
Home then, and weep as mothers weep

Over their sickly babes asleep.——
Why did my soul in flesh take breath,
If love of flesh is the soul's death?——
Stay near me, priest!——I am not clear
How I shall feel when death is near.
" Naked into the grave descend,"——
I'll wait, at least, until the end.　　　[*Goes.*

BRAND.
[*Gazing after her.*]
Yes, thy son shall still be near,
Call to him, and he shall hear.
Stretch thy hand, and, cold and perish'd,
At his heart it shall be cherish'd.
　　　[*Goes down to* AGNES.]
As the Morn not so the Night.
Then my soul was set on fight,
Then I heard the war-drum rattle,
Yearn'd the sword of Wrath to swing,
Lies to trample, Trolls to fling,
Fill the world with clashing battle.

AGNES.
[*Has turned round to him, and looks radiantly up.*]
By the Night the Morn was pale.
Then I sought the joys that fail;
Sought to triumph by attaining
What in losing I am gaining.

BRAND.
Visions stirring, visions splendid
Like a flock of swans descended,
On their spreading wings upbore me,
And I saw my way before me;——
Sin-subduer of the Age

Sternly stemming seas that rage.
Church-processions, banners streaming,
Anthems rolling, incense steaming
Golden goblets, victor-songs,
Rapt applause of surging throngs,
Made a glory where I fought.
All in dazzling hues was wrought ;—
Yet it was an empty dream,
A brief mountain-vision, caught
Half in glare and half in gleam.
   Now I stand where twilight gray
Long forestalls the ebb of day,
'Twixt the water and the wild,
From the busy world exiled,
Just a strip of heaven's blue dome
Visible ;—but this is Home.
Now my Sabbath dream is dark ;
To the stall my winged steed ;
But I see a higher Mark.
Than to wield the knightly sabre,—
Daily duty, daily labour,
Hallow'd to a Sabbath-deed.

AGNES.

And that God, who was to fall ?

BRAND.

He shall, none the less, be fell'd,—
But in secret, unbeheld,
Not before the eyes of all.
Now I see, I judged astray
Where the Folk's salvation lay.
Not by high heroic charges
Can you make the People whole ;
That which faculty enlarges
Does not heal the fissured soul.

It is Will alone that matters
Will alone that mars or makes,
Will, that no distraction scatters,
And that no resistance breaks.——
[*Turns towards the hamlet, where the shades of night
are beginning to fall.*]
Come then, Men, who downcast roam
The pent valley of my home ;——
Close conversing we will try
Our own souls to purify,
Slackness curb and falsehood kill,
Rouse the lion's cub of Will !
Manly, as the hands that smite,
Are the hands that hold the hoe ;
There's one end for all,—to grow
Tablets whereon God may write.
     [*He is going.* EINAR *confronts him.*

EINAR.

Stand, and what you took restore !

BRAND.

Is it she ? You see her there.

EINAR.
[*To* AGNES.]
Choose between the sunny shore
And this savage den of care.

AGNES.

There I have no choice to make.

EINAR.

Agnes, Agnes, hear me yet !
The old saying you forget,
Light to lift and hard to bear.

AGNES.

Go with God, thou tempter fair ;
I shall bear until I break.

EINAR.

For thy mother's, sisters' sake !

AGNES.

Bring my greetings to my Home ;
I will write—if words should come.

EINAR.

Over ocean's gleaming breast
White sails hurry from the strand ;—
Like the sighs of dreaming brows,
Lofty, diamond-beaded prows
Speed them to their haven-rest
In a far-off vision'd land.

AGNES.

Sail to westward, sail to east ;—
Think of me as one deceased.

EINAR.

As a sister come with me.

AGNES.
[*Shaking her head.*]
'Twixt us rolls a boundless sea.

EINAR.

O, then homeward to thy mother !

AGNES.
[*Softly.*]
Not from Master, Friend, and Brother.

BRAND.
[Coming a step nearer.]
Youthful maiden, weigh it well.
In this mountain-prison pent,
Oversoar'd by crag and fell,
In this dim and yawning rent,
Life henceforward shall be gray
As an ebbing autumn-day.

AGNES.
Gloom appals no more ; afar
Through the cloud-wrack gleams a star.

BRAND.
Know, that I am stern to crave,
All or Nothing I will have ;
If that call you disobey,
You have flung your life away.
No abatement in distress,
And for sin no tenderness,—
If life's service God refuse,
Life you joyfully must lose.

EINAR.
Fly this wild insensate play !
Spurn the sullen Doomer's sway ;
Live the life you know you may !

BRAND.
At the crossway standst thou :—choose.
                                              [Goes.

EINAR.
Choose the stillness or the strife !
For the choice to go or stay
Is a choice of calm or fray,

Is a choice of Night or Day,
Is a choice of Death or Life !

AGNES.

[*Rises, and then says slowly :*]
On through Death.   On into Night.——
Dawn beyond glows rosy-bright.
  [*She follows, where* BRAND *has gone.* EINAR
  *gazes a moment in bewilderment after
  her, then bows his head, and goes back to
  the fjord.*

ACT THIRD.

*Three years later.   A little garden by the Parsonage.
A great precipice above, a stone wall round.
The fjord, narrow and pent in, appears in the
background.   The house-door opens upon the
garden.   Afternoon.*
BRAND *is standing on the steps outside the house.*
AGNES *is sitting on the step at his feet.*

AGNES.
My dearest husband, still your eye
Over the fjord roves anxiously—

BRAND.
I wait a summons.

AGNES.
With brows bent!

BRAND.
My Mother's summons.   This three years
I've waited between hopes and fears
The summons that was never sent.
To-day 'twas told me, past a doubt,
That her life's span is almost out.

AGNES.
[*Softly and tenderly.*]
Brand, without summons you should go?

BRAND.
[*Shakes his head.*]
Till she of her offence repent
I have no comfort to bestow.

AGNES.
She is your mother .

BRAND.
                    It were sin
To worship idols in my kin.

AGNES.
Brand, you are stern !

BRAND.
                    To you ?

AGNES.
                              Oh no

BRAND.
I warn'd you that the way was steep.

AONES.
[*Smiling.*]
It was not true ; you did not keep
Your word.

BRAND.
                    Yes, here the ice-wind rives ;
Your cheek has lost its youthful glow,
Your tender heart is touch'd with snow.
Our home is built where nothing thrives,
Amid a barren waste of stone.

AGNES.
It lies the safer, then !   So prone
Beetles yon jutting mountain-wall,

That, when the leafy spring is near,
The brimming avalanche vaults sheer
Over our heads, and we lie clear
As in the hollow of a fall.

BRAND.

The sun we never see at all.

AGNES.

Oh, yet he dances warm and bright
Atop yon mountain that we face.

BRAND.

For three weeks, true,—at summer's height,—
But never struggles to its base !

AGNES.

[*Looks fixedly at him, rises and says.*]
Brand, there's one thought at which you shrink.

BRAND.

No, you !

AGNES.

No, you !

BRAND.

Within you bear
A secret terror.

AGNES.

Which you share !

BRAND.

You reel as from a dizzy brink !
Out with it ! speak it out !

AGNES.

'Tis true
I've trembled, whiles—— [*Hesitates*

III F

BRAND.

      Trembled !   At what !

AGNES.

For Alf.

BRAND.

   For Alf ?

AGNES.

    And so have you !

BRAND.

At times.   But no, God takes him not !
God's merciful !   My child shall grow
To be a strong man yet, I know.
Where is he now ?

AGNES.

   He's sleeping.

BRAND.

[*Looks in through the door.*]
         See ;
Of pain and grief he dreams not, he ;
The little hand is plump and round——

AGNES.

Yet pale.

BRAND.

  But that will pass.

AGNES.

     How deep,
Restful and quickening is his sleep.

BRAND.

God bless thee ; in thy sleep grow sound !
[*Shuts the door.*]

To all my labours you and he
Have brought light and tranquillity ;
Each irksome task, each mournful care,
'Twas easy, in your midst, to bear ;
You near, I never felt dismay,
Grew braver by his baby-play.
A martyrdom I held my Call,
But something has transform'd it all,—
Success still follows my footfall.

AGNES.

Yes, Brand ; but you deserve success.
Oh, you have battled, in storm and stress ;—
Toil'd on through woe and weariness ;—
But tears of blood you wept, apart——

BRAND.

And yet it seem'd so light a thing ;
With you, love stole upon my heart
Like a glad sunny day in Spring.
In me Love never had been lit ;
No parents' hand had kindled it,
Rather they quench'd the fitful flashes
That gleam'd at moments in the ashes.
It was as though the tender Soul
That mute and darkling in me slept,
Had, closely garner'd, all been kept
To be my sweet Wife's aureole.

AGNES.

Not mine alone : but whosoe'er
In our great Household has a share,
Each sorrowing son, each needy brother,
Each weeping child, each mourning mother,
Of quickening nurture have their part,
At the rich banquet of thy heart.

BRAND.

Only through you two.   By your hand
That heavenly bridge of love was spann'd;
No single soul can all contain
Except it first have yearn'd for one.
I had to long and yearn in vain,
So my heart harden'd into stone.

AGNES.

And yet—your love is merciless;
You chasten whom you would caress.

BRAND.

You, Agnes?

AGNES.

            Me?   O nay, dear, nay!
On me a lightsome load you lay.
But many falter at the call
To offer Nothing or else all.

BRAND.

What the world calls by that name "Love,
I know not and I reck not of.
God's love _I_ recognise alone,
Which melts not at the piteous plaint,
Which is not moved by dying groan,
And its caress is chastisement.
What answer'd through the olive-trees
God, when the Son in anguish lay,
Praying, "O take this cup away!"
Did He then take it?   Nay, child, nay:
He made him drink it to the lees.

AGNES.

By such a measure meted, all
The souls of earth are forfeited.

BRAND.

None knows on whom the doom shall fall;
But God in flaming speech hath said :
" Be faithful through the hour of strife :
Haggling wins not the crown of life ! "
Anguish'd repentance scales not heaven,
The martyr's doom you must fulfil.
That you lack'd strength may be forgiven,—
But never that you wanted will.

AGNES.

Yes, it shall be as you have said ;
O lift me to those heights you tread ;
To your high heaven lead me forth,
My spirit is strong, my flesh is frail ;
Oft, anguish-struck, I faint, I fail,—
My clogg'd foot drags upon the earth.

BRAND.

See, child ; of all men God makes one
Demand : No coward compromise !
Whose work's half done or falsely done,
Condemn'd with God his whole word lies.
We must give sanction to this teaching
By living it and not by preaching.

AGNES
[*Throws herself on his neck.*]
Lead where you will ; I follow you !

BRAND.
No precipice is too steep for two.

Enter the DOCTOR ; *he has come down the road, and
stops outside the garden fence*

THE DOCTOR.

Ha! loving doves at their caresses
In these dark craggy wildernesses?

AGNES.

My dear old Doctor, here at last!
Come in, come in!
                    [*Runs down and opens the garden gate.*

THE DOCTOR.
                    Ho, not so fast!
We've first to settle an old score.—
What!   Tie yourself to this wild moor,
Where piercing winds of winter tear
Like ice, soul, body to the core——

BRAND.

Not soul.

THE DOCTOR.
                    Not?   Well, I must admit,
That seems about the truth of it.
Your hasty compact has an air
Of standing firm, unmoved, erect,
Though otherwise, one might expect,
By ancient usage, soon to fade
That which so suddenly was made.

AGNES.

A sunbeam's kiss, a bell's note, may
Awaken for a summer's day.

THE DOCTOR.

A patient waits for me. Farewell.

BRAND.

My mother?

THE DOCTOR.
Yes.   You also go?

BRAND.
Not now.

THE DOCTOR.
Have been, I daresay?

BRAND.
No.

THE DOCTOR.
Priest, you are hard.   Through mist and snow
I've trudged across the desolate fell,
Well knowing that she is of those
Who pay like paupers.

BRAND.
May God bless
Your skill and your unweariedness!
Ease, if you can, her bitter throes.

THE DOCTOR.
Bless my goodwill! I tarried not
A moment when I heard her state.

BRAND.
You she has summon'd : I'm forgot,—
And sick at heart, I wait, I wait.

THE DOCTOR.
Come without summons!

BRAND.
Till she calls,
I have no place within those walls.

THE DOCTOR.
[*To* AGNES.]
You hapless blossom, laid within
The pitiless grasp of such a lord!

BRAND.
I am not pitiless.

AGNES.
He had pour'd
His blood, to wash her soul from sin

BRAND.
Unask'd, upon myself I took
The clearance of her debit-book.

THE DOCTOR.
Clear off your own!

BRAND.
One man may get
Hundreds acquitted, in God's eyes.

THE DOCTOR.
Ay; not a Beggar though, who lies
Himself o'er head and ears in debt.

BRAND.
Beggar or rich,—with all my soul
I will;—and that one thing's the whole

THE DOCTOR.
Yes, in you ledger, truly, Will
Has enough entries and to spare:
But, priest, your Love-account is still
A virgin-chapter, blank and bare.   [*Goes.*

BRAND.

[Follows him awhile with his eyes.]

Never did word so sorely prove
The smirch of lies, as this word Love :
With devilish craft, where will is frail,
Men lay Love over, as a veil,
And cunningly conceal thereby
That all their life is coquetry.
Whose path's the steep and perilous slope,
Let him but love,—and he may shirk it ;
If he prefer Sin's easy circuit,
Let him but love,—he still may hope ;
If God he seeks, but fears the fray,
Let him but love,—'tis straight his prey ;
If with wide-open eyes he err,
Let him but love,—there's safety there !

AGNES.

Yes, it is false : yet still I fall
Questioning : Is it, after all ?

BRAND.

One point's omitted : First the Will
Law's thirst for righteousness must still.
You must first will ! Not only things
Attainable, in more or less,
Nor only where the action brings
Some hardship and some weariness ;
No, you must will with flashing eyes
Your way through all earth's agonies.
It is not martyrdom to toss
In anguish on the deadly cross :
But to have will'd to perish so,
To will it through each bodily throe,
To will it with still-tortured mind,
This, only this, redeems mankind.

AGNES.

[*Clinging closely to him.*]

If at the terrible call I cower,
Speak, strong-soul'd husband, in that hour!

BRAND.

If Will has conquer'd in that strife,
Then comes at length the hour of Love;
Then it descends like a white dove,
Bearing the olive-leaf of life:
But in this nerveless, slothful state,
The true, the sovereign Love is—Hate!
                    [*In horror.*]
Hate! Hate! O Titan's toil, to will
That one brief easy syllable!

                    [*Goes hurriedly into the house.*

AGNES.

[*Looking through the open door.*]

He kneels beside his little son,
And heaves as if with bursts of tears;
He clutches close the bed, like one
That knows no refuge from his fears.—
O what a wealth of tender ruth
Lies hidden in this breast of steel!
Alf he dares love: the baby-heel
Has not yet felt Earth's serpent-tooth.
                    [*Cries out in terror.*]
Ha! he leaps up with ashy brow!
Wringing his hands! what sees he now

BRAND.

[*Coming out.*]

A summons came?

AGNES.

No summons, no

BRAND.

[*Looking back into the house.*]
His parch'd skin burns in fever-glow;
His temples throb, his pulses race———!
Oh fear not, Agnes!

AGNES.

God of grace———

BRAND.

Nay, have no fear———
[*Calls out over the road.*]
The summons, see.

A MAN.

[*Through the garden-gate.*]
You must come now, priest!

BRAND.

Instantly!
What message?

THE MAN.

A mysterious one.
Sitting in bed she forward bent,
And said: "Get the priest here: begone!
My half-goods for the sacrament."

BRAND.

[*Starts back.*]
Her half-goods! No! Say no!

THE MAN.
[*Shakes his head.*]
                   My word
Would then not utter what I heard.

BRAND.
Half! Half! It was the whole she meant!

THE MAN.
Maybe ; but she spoke loud and high ;
And I don't easily forget.

BRAND.
[*Seizes his arm.*]
Before God's Judgment, will you yet
Dare to attest she spoke it ?

THE MAN.
                Ay.

BRAND.
[*Firmly.*]
Go, tell her, this reply was sent :
" Nor priest shall come, nor sacrament."

THE MAN.
[*Looking at him doubtfully.*]
You surely have not understood
It is your Mother that appeals.

BRAND.
I know no law that sternlier deals
With strangers than with kindred blood.

THE MAN,
A hard word, that.

BRAND.

                She knows the call,—
To offer Nothing, or else all.

THE MAN.

Priest !

BRAND.

        Dock the gold-calf as she will,
Say, it remains an idol still.

THE MAN.

The scourge you send her I will lay
As gently on her as I may.
She has this comfort left her, too :
God is not quite so hard as you !   -[*Goes.*

BRAND.

Yes, with that comfort's carrion-breath
The world still sickens unto death ;
Prompt, in its need, with shriek and song
To lubricate the Judge's tongue.
Of course !   The reasonable plan !
For from of old they know their man ;—
Since all his works the assurance breathe :
" Yon gray-beard may be haggled with ! "
        [THE MAN *has met another man on the road;
        they come back together.*

BRAND.

A second message '

FIRST MAN.
Yes.

BRAND.
[To *the* SECOND MAN.]
                Consent !

SECOND MAN.

Nine-tenths of it is now the word.

BRAND.

Not all ?

SECOND MAN.

Not all.

BRAND.

As you have heard :—
Nor priest shall come, nor sacrament.

SECOND MAN.

She begg'd it, bitterly distress'd——

FIRST MAN.

Priest, once she bore you on her breast .

BRAND.
[*Clenching his hands.*]

I may not by two measures weigh
My kinsman and my enemy.

SECOND MAN.

Sore is her state and dire her need ;
Come, or else send her a God-speed

BRAND.
[*To* FIRST MAN.]

Go ; tell her still : God's wine and bread
Must on a spotless board be spread.

[*The Men go.*

AGNES.

I tremble Brand.   You seem a Sword
Swung flaming by a wrathful Lord !

BRAND.

[*With tears in his voice.*]

Does not the world face me no less
With swordless sheath upon its thigh?
Am I not torn and baffled by
Its dull defiant stubbornness?

AGNES.

A hard condition you demand.

BRAND.

Dare you impose a lighter?

AGNES.

Lay
That stern demand on whom you may,
And see who, tested so, will stand.

BRAND.

Nay, you have reason for that fear.
So base, distorted, barren, sere,
The aspiring soul in men is grown.
'Tis thought a marvel,—by bequest
To give away one's wealth unknown.
And be anonymously bless'd.
The hero, bid him blot his name,
Content him with the service wrought,
Kings, Kaisers, bid him do the same—
And see how many fields are fought!
The poet, bid him unbeholden
Loose his bright fledglings from the cage,
So that none dream he gave that golden
Plumage, and he that vocal rage;
Try the green bough, or try the bare,
Sacrifice is not anywhere.
Earth has enslaved all earthly things;—

Over Life's precipices cast,
Each to its mouldering branches clings,
And, if they crumble, clutches fast
With tooth and nail to straws and bast

AGNES.

And, while they helpless, hopeless fall,
You cry : Give nothing or give all '

BRAND.

He who would conquer still must fight,
Rise, fallen to the highest height.
      [*A brief silence : his voice changes.*]
And yet, when with that stern demand
Before some living soul I stand,
I seem like one that floats afar
Storm-shatter'd on a broken spar.
With solitary anguish wrung
I've bitten this chastising tongue,
And thirsted, as I aim'd the blow,
To clasp the bosom of my foe.
   Go, Agnes, watch the sleeping boy,
And sing him into dreams of joy.
An infant's soul is like the sleep
Of still clear tarns in summer-light.
A mother over it may sweep
And hover, like the bird, whose flight
Is mirror'd in the deepest deep.

AGNES.

What does it mean, Brand ? Wheresoe'er
You aim your thought-shafts—they fly there!

BRAND.

Oh, nothing. Softly watch the child.

AGNES.

Give me a watchword.

BRAND.

Stern ?

AGNES.

No, mild.

BRAND.

[*Clasping her.*]

The blameless shall not taste the grave.

AGNES.

[*Looking brightly up at him.*]

Then one is ours God may not crave !

[*Goes into the house.*

BRAND.

[*Looking fixedly before him.*]

But if he might ?   What " Isaac's Fear "
Once ventured, He may venture here.

[*Shakes off the thought.*]

No, no, my sacrifice is made,
The calling of my life gainsaid—
Like the Lord's thunder to go forth
And rouse the sleepers of the earth.
Sacrifice !   Liar ! there was none !
I miss'd it when my Dream was done,
When Agnes woke me—and follow'd free
To labour in the gloom with me.

[*Looks along the road.*]

Why tarries still the dying call,
Her word, that she will offer all,
That she has won that which uproots
Sin's deepest fibres, rankest shoots !
See there——— !   No, it is but the Mayor,
Well-meaning, brisk, and debonnaire,

III   G

Both hands in pockets, round, remiss,
A bracketed parenthesis.

Enter MAYOR.

THE MAYOR.
[*Through the garden gate.*]
Good-day!   Our meetings are but rare,
Perhaps my time is chosen amiss——

BRAND.
[*Pointing to house.*]
Come in.

THE MAYOR.
            Thanks ; here I'm quite content.
Should my proposal meet assent,
I'm very sure the upshot of it
Would issue in our common profit.

BRAND.
Name your desire.

THE MAYOR.
                Your mother's state,
I understand, is desperate.
I'm sorry.

BRAND.
That I do not doubt.

THE MAYOR.
I'm very sorry.

BRAND.
Pray, speak out.

THE MAYOR.
She's old, however.   Welladay,
We are all bound the selfsame way —

And, as I just drove by, occurr'd
The thought that, after all, " to leap
Is just as easy as to creep " :
Moreover, many have averr'd,
That she and you have been imbrued
For years in a domestic feud——

BRAND.

Domestic feud ?

THE MAYOR.

　　　　　She's out and out
Close-fisted, so they say, you know.
You think it goes too far, no doubt.
A man's own claims he can't forego.
She keeps exclusive occupation
Of all that was bequeath'd to you.

BRAND.

Exclusive occupation, true.

THE MAYOR.

A ready cause of irritation
In families.　Surmising thence
That you await with resignation
The moment of her going hence,
I hope I may without offence
Speak out, although I quite admit
The time I've chosen is unfit.

BRAND.

Or now or later, nought I care.

THE MAYOR.

Well, to the point then, fair and square.
When once your mother's dead and blest,
In the earth's bosom laid to rest,
You're rich !

BRAND.

You think so?

THE MAYOR.

            Think?   Nay, man,
That's sure.   She's land in every port,
Far as a telescope can scan.
You're rich!

BRAND.

'Spite the Succession Court?

THE MAYOR.
[*Smiling.*]
What of it?   That cuts matters short
When many fight for pelf and debt.
Here no man's interest suffers let.

BRAND.

And what if some day, all the same,
Came a co-heir to debt and pelf
Crying: "I'm he!" and urged his claim?

THE MAYOR.

He'd have to be the devil himself!
Just look to me!   None else has here
The smallest right to interfere.
I know my business: lean on me!
Well, then; you'll now be well-to-do,
Rich even; you'll no longer brook
Life in this God-forsaken nook;
The whole land's open now to you.

BRAND.

Mayor, is not what you want to say,
Pithily put, just: "Go away'?

THE MAYOR.

Pretty much that.   All parties' good
Were so best answered.   If you would
But eye attentively the herd
To whom you minister God's word,
You'd find you're no more of a piece
With them than foxes are with geese.
Pray, understand me !   You have gifts,
Good where the social field is wide,
But dangerous for folk whose pride
Is to be Lords of rocky rifts
And Freemen of the ravine-side.

BRAND.

To a man's feet his native haunt
Is as unto the tree the root.
If there his labour fill no want
His deeds are doomed, his music mute.

THE MAYOR.

Success means just : Self-adaptation
To the requirements of the nation.

BRAND.

Which from the heights you best o'erlook,
Not from the crag-encompass'd nook.

THE MAYOR.

That talk is fit for citizens,
Not for poor peasants of the glens.

BRAND.

O, still your limitation vain
Between the mountain and the plain !
World-citizens you'd be of right,
While every civic claim you slight ;
And think, like dastards, to go free
By whining : "We're a small folk, we ! "

THE MAYOR.

All has its time, each time its need,
Each age its proper work to do ;
We also flung our mite into
The world's great treasure of bold deed.
True, that's long since ; but, after all,
The mite was not so very small.
Now the land's dwindled and decay'd,
But our renown still lives in story.
The days of our reported glory
Were when the great King Belë sway'd.
Many a tale is still related
About the brothers Wulf and Thor,
And gallant fellows by the score,
Went harrying to the British shore,
And plunder'd till their heart was sated.
The Southrons shriek'd with quivering lip,
" Lord, help us from these fierce men's grip,"
And these " fierce men," beyond all doubt,
Had from our harbours sallied out.
And how these rovers wreak'd their ire,
And dealt out death with sword and fire !
Nay, legend names a lion-hearted
Hero that took the cross ; in verity,
It is not mention'd that he started——

BRAND.

He left behind a large posterity,
This promise-maker ?

THE MAYOR.
                        Yes, indeed ;
But how came you to—— ?

BRAND.
                        O, I read
His features clearly in the breed

Of promise-heroes of to-day,
Who take the Cross in just his way.

THE MAYOR.

Yes, his descendants still remain.
But we were on King Belë's reign!
So first abroad we battled.   Then,
Visited our own countrymen
And kinsmen, with the axe and fire ;
Trampled their harvests gaily down,
Scorch'd mansion-wall and village spire,
And wove ourselves the hero's crown.—
Over the blood thus set a-flowing
There's been perhaps excessive crowing;
But, after what I've said, I may,
I think, without a touch of vanity,
Point backward to the stir we made
In the great Age long since decay'd,
And hold that we indeed have paid
Our little mite of Fire and Fray
Towards the Progress of Humanity.

BRAND.

Yet do you not, in fact, eschew
The phrase, " Nobility's a trust,"—
And drive hoe, plough, and harrow through
King Belë's patrimonial dust?

THE MAYOR.

By no means.   Only go and mark
Our parish on its gaudy-nights,
Where I with Constable and Clerk,
And Judge, preside as leading lights ;
You'll warrant, when the punch goes round,
King Belë's memory is sound.
With toasts and clinking cups and song,
In speeches short and speeches long,

We drink his health and sound his fame.
I myself often feel inclined
The spinnings of my brain to wind
In flowery woof about his name,
And edify the local mind.
A little poetry pleases me,
And all our folks, in their degree ;
But—moderation everywhere !
In life it never must have share,—
Except at night, when folks have leisure,
Between the hours of seven and ten,
When baths of elevating pleasure
May fit the mood of weary men.
Here's where we differ, you and we,
That you desire with main and might
At the same time to plough and fight.
Your scheme, as far as I can see,
Is : Life and Faith in unity,—
God's warfare and potato-dressing
Inseparably coalescing,
As coal, salt, sulphur, fusing fast,
Evolve just gunpowder at last.

BRAND.

Somewhat so.

THE MAYOR.

       Here you'll scheme in vain !
Out in the great world that may stand ;—
Go thither with your big demand,
And let us plough our moors and main.

BRAND.

Plough first your brag of old renown
Into the main, and plough it down !
The pigmy is not more the man
For being of Goliath's clan.

THE MAYOR.

Great memories bear the seed of growth.

BRAND.

Yes, memories that to life are bound;
But you, of memory's empty mound,
Have made a stalking-horse for sloth.

THE MAYOR.

I said at first, and still I say :—
To leave us were the wisest way.
Your work here cannot come to good,
Nor your ideas be understood.
The little flights to purer air,
The lifting-up which, now and then,
Is doubtless well for working men,
Shall be my unremitting care.
Many agreeable facts declare
My ceaseless energy as mayor,—
Through me the population's grown
Double, nay, almost three to one,
Since for the district I have bred
Ever new ways of getting fed.
With stubborn nature still at strife
We've steam'd ahead : our forward march
Here hew'd a road, there flung an arch—
To lead from——

BRAND.

   Not from Faith to Life.

THE MAYOR.

To lead from fjordside to the hill.

BRAND.

But not from Doctrine unto Will.

THE MAYOR.

First of all, get a passage clear
From men to men, from place to place.
There were no two opinions here
On that, until you show'd your face.
Now you've made all confusion, dashing
Aurora-flames with lantern light ;
With such cross-luminaries flashing,
Who can distinguish wrong from right,
Tell what will mar, and what will mend ?
All diverse things you mix and blend,
And into hostile camps divide
Those who should triumph side by side.

BRAND.

Here, notwithstanding, I abide.
Man chooses not his labour's sphere.
Who knows and follows out his call,
Has seen God's writing on the wall,
In words of fire, " Your place is here ! "

THE MAYOR.

Stay, then, but keep within your borders ;
You're free to purge the folk of crimes,
Vices, and other rifle disorders ;
God knows, it's needed oftentimes !
But don't make every working-day
A Sabbath, and your flag display,
As if the Almighty were on board
Of every skiff that skims the fjord.

BRAND.

To use your counsel, I must change
My soul and all her vision's range ;
But we are called, ourselves to be,

Our own cause bear to victory ;
And I will bear it, till the land
Is all illumined where I stand !
The people, your bureaucrat-crew
Have lull'd asleep, shall wake anew ;
Too long you've cramp'd and caged apart
These remnants of the Mountain heart ;
Out of your niggard hunger-cure
They pass dejected, dull, demure :
Their best, their bravest blood you tap,
Scoop out their marrow and their sap,
Pound into splinters every soul,
That should have stood a welded whole ;—
But you may live to hear the roar
Of revolution thunder : War !

THE MAYOR.
War ?

BRAND.
War !

THE MAYOR.
Be sure, if you should call
To arms, you'll be the first to fall.

BRAND.
The day will come when we shall know
That triumph's height is Overthrow.

THE MAYOR.
Consider, Brand, you have to choose !
Don't stake your fortune on one card.

BRAND.
I do, however !

THE MAYOR.

If you lose,
Your life's irreparably marr'd.
All this world's bounties you possess,
You, a rich Mother's only heir,
With wife and child to be your care,—
It was a kindly hand, confess,
That dealt your terms of happiness!

BRAND.

And what if I should, all the same,
Reject these terms? and must?

THE MAYOR.

      Your game
Is over, if you've once unfurl'd
In this last cranny of the world
The standard of your world-wide war.
Turn southward, to yon prosperous shore
Where a man dares lift up his head;
There you may perorate of right
And bid them bleed and bid them fight;
Our bloodshed is the sweat we pour
In daily wringing rocks for bread.

BRAND.

Here I remain. My home is here!
And here the battle-flag I'll rear.

THE MAYOR.

Think what you lose, if overthrown,
And, chiefly, think of what you quit!

BRAND.

Myself I lose, if I submit.

THE MAYOR.

Hopeless is he that fights alone.

BRAND.

The best are with me.

THE MAYOR.
[*Smiling.*]
That may be,
But they're the most, who follow me.

[*Goes.*

BRAND
[*Looking after him.*]
A people's champion, thorough-bred!
Active, with fair and open hand,
Honest of heart and sound of head,
But yet a scourge upon the land !
No avalanche, no winter-blast,
No flood, nor frost, nor famine-fast
Leaves half the ruin in its rear
That such a man does, year by year.
Life only by a plague is reft;
But he——!　How many a thought is cleft,
How many an eager will made numb,
How many a valiant song struck dumb
By such a narrow soul as this!
What smiles on simple faces breaking,
What fires in lowly bosoms waking,
What pangs of joy and anger, seed
That might have ripened into deed,
Die by that bloodless blade of his !
[*Suddenly, in anxiety.*]
But O the summons ! the summons —No'
It is the Doctor !

Enter Doctor.

[*Hurries to meet him.*]
                Say ! say ! How———— ?

THE DOCTOR.
She stands before her Maker now.

BRAND.
Dead !—But repentant ?

THE DOCTOR.
                    Scarcely so ;
She hugg'd Earth's goods with all her heart
Till the Hour struck, and they must part.

BRAND.
[*Looking straight before him in deep emotion.*]
Is here an erring soul undone ?

THE DOCTOR.
She will be mildly judged, maybe ;——
And Law temper'd with equity,

BRAND.
[*In a low tone.*]
What said she ?

THE DOCTOR.
                Low she mutter'd : He
Is no hard dealer, like my son.

BRAND.
[*Sinking in anguish upon the bench*]
Guilt-wrung or dying, still that lie
That every soul is ruin'd by !
                [*Hides his face in his hands.*

The Doctor.

[Goes towards him, looks at him, and shakes his head.]

You seek, a day that is no more,
In one and all things to restore.
You think, God's venerable pact
With man is still a living fact;—
Each Age in its own way will walk;
Ours is not scared by nurses' talk
Of hell-bound soul and burning brand;—
Humanity's our first command!

Brand.
[Looking up.]

Humanity!—That sluggard phrase
Is the world's watchword nowadays.
With this each bungler hides the fact
That he dare not and will not act;
With this each weakling masks the lie,
That he'll risk all for victory;
With this each dastard dares to cloak
Vows faintly rued and lightly broke;
Your puny spirits will turn Man
Himself Humanitarian!
Was God " humane " when Jesus died?
Had your God then his counsel given,
Christ at the cross for grace had cried—
And the Redemption signified
A diplomatic note from Heaven.

[Hides his head, and sits in mute grief.

The Doctor.
[Softly.]

Rage, rage thy fill, thou soul storm-stress'd ;—
Best were it for thee to find tears.

AGNES.

[*Comes out on to the steps: pale and terrified she whispers to the* DOCTOR.]

In! Follow me!

THE DOCTOR.

You raise my fears!
What is it, child?

AGNES.

Into my breast
Creeps cold a serpent of affright——!

THE DOCTOR.

What is it?

AGNES.

[*Pulling him away.*]
Come!—Great God of Might.

[*They go into the house;* BRAND *does not notice.*

BRAND.

[*To himself.*]
Impenitent alive,—and dead!
This is the finger of the Lord!
Now through my means shall be restored
The treasure she has forfeited;
Else tenfold woe upon my head!

[*Rises.*]
Henceforth as by my sonship bound,
Unflinching, on my native ground
I'll battle, a soldier of the Cross,
For Spirit's gain by Body's loss.
Me with His purging fire the Lord
Hath arm'd, and with His riving Word:
Mine is that Will and that strong Trust
That crumbles mountains into dust!

The Doctor.
[*Followed by* Agnes *comes hastily out, and cries.*]
Order your house and haste away !

Brand.
Were there an earthquake I would stay !

The Doctor.
Then you have doom'd your child to death.

Brand.
[*Wildly.*]
The child ! Alf ! Alf ! What phantom wraith
Of fear is this ! My child !
　　　　　　　[*Is about to rush into the house.*

The Doctor.
[*Holding him back.*]
　　　　　　　　Stay, stay .—
Here summer sunshine pierces not,
Here polar ice-blasts rive and rend,—
Here dank and stifling mists descend.
Another winter in this spot
Will shrivel the tender life away.
Go hence, you'll save him ! No delay !
To-morrow's best.

Brand.
　　　　　　To-night,—to-day !
Now, ere another hour is out !
O yet he shall grow strong and stout ;—
No blast from mountain or from shore
Shall chill his baby-bosom more.
Come, Agnes, lift him gently in sleep !
Away along the winding deep !

O Agnes, Agnes, death has spun
His web about our little son !

AGNES.

Foreboding trembled in my heart,—
And yet I only knew a part.

BRAND.
[*To the* DOCTOR.]
But flight will save him ?   That is sure ?

THE DOCTOR.

The life a father day and night
Watches, all perils can endure.
Be all to him ! and healthy, bright,
You soon shall see him, be secure !

BRAND.

Thanks, thanks !
[*To* AGNES.]
In down enclose him well ;
Chill sweeps the night-wind from the fell.
[AGNES *goes in.*

The DOCTOR *silently watches* BRAND, *who gazes
fixedly through the door ; then goes to him, and
lays his hand on his shoulder.*

THE DOCTOR.

So tender to his own distress.
And to the world so merciless !
For them avails not more nor less !
Only Law's absolute Nought or All,
But now——no sooner sees he fall
The dooming lot,—his valour's flown ;
——The sacrificial lamb's his own !

BRAND.
What mean you ?

THE DOCTOR.
                              In the dying ear
You thunder'd the decree of fear :
To perish, unless All she gave,
And went down naked to her grave !
And that cry rang again, again,
When need was direst among men !
You're now the shipwreckt sailor, cleaving
To swamp'd boat through the storms of doom,
And from its upturn'd bottom heaving
To see your tracts on Wrath to Come,
To sea, to sea, the bulky tome
That struck your Brothers' bosoms home ;
Now you ask only wind and wave
To waft your infant from death's reach.
Fly, only fly, by bay and beach,
Fly from your very mother's grave,—
Fly from the souls you're sent to save ;—
" The Parson does not mean to preach !"

BRAND.
[*Wildly clutching his head as if to gather his thoughts.*
Am I now blind ?   Or was I ?

THE DOCTOR.
                                        Nay,
A father has no other way ;
Don't fancy that your act I blame ;
I hold you greater, clipt and tame,
Than in your giant strength secure.—
Farewell ! I've held you up a glass ;
Use it and sigh : " Alas, alas,
Is this a Titan's portraiture ?"   [*Goes.*

BRAND.

Gazing a while before him : then bursts out.]
Before—or now,—when did I stray ?

AGNES *comes out with a cloak over her shoulders*
and the child in her arms ; BRAND does not see
her ; she is about to speak, but stands petrified
with terror at the look in his face. At the same
moment A MAN comes in hastily through the
garden-gate. The sun is setting.

THE MAN.

Hark, priest, you have a foe !

BRAND.

[Clenching his hand against his breast.]
                                        Yes, here!

THE MAN.

Watch well the Mayor. The seed you sow
Sprang ever bravely into ear,
Till blighting slanders laid it low.
With meaning hints he has implied
That by-and-by this house would lack
A tenant, and you'd turn your back,
The day your wealthy mother died.

BRAND.

And if it were so——

THE MAN.

                    Priest, I know you ;
Know, why these poisonous tales are rife ;
You stood against him still at strife ;
He could not bend your purpose :—lo, you,
That's what these slanders signified——

BRAND.

[*Hesitating.*]

Suppose the case—that he spoke true?

THE MAN.

Then to us all you've basely lied.

BRAND.

Have I——— ?

THE MAN.

How oft you've told us, you,
That God has call'd you to the strife,
That here you've made your home for life,
That here you'll bear the battle through,
That none may shirk the call to serve,
That all must fight and never swerve,
You have the Call! How flames and flashes
In many a heart the fire you've fed!

BRAND.

This people's heart is hard and dead!
Their ear is deaf, their fire is ashes!

THE MAN.

O, you know better;—radiant day
To many a heart has found its way.

BRAND.

In tenfold others all is night.

THE MAN.

You're sent to be their beacon-light
But be the numbers as you choose,
Here is no need to closely scan;
For here I stand, one only Man,

And bid you : Leave us, if you can !
I have a soul I would not lose,
Like others ; books I cannot use,
You bore me from the depths below,—
Try if you now can let me go !
You cannot,—I so closely grip,
My soul were lost if I should slip.
Farewell ; I look to learn at last :
My priest by me—and God—stands fast .

                       [*Goes.*

AGNES.
[*Timidly.*]
Your lips are blanch'd, and white your cheek ;
You seem to utter an inward shriek !

BRAND.
Each strong word flung at yonder rock
Thrills back with tenfold echo's shock.

AGNES.
[*Advancing a step.*]
I'm ready !

BRAND.
Ready ?   Whereunto ?

AGNES.
[*Vehemently.*]
For what a mother needs must do !

GERD.
[*Runs by outside and stops at the garden-gate ;
claps her hands and cries in wild joy.*]
Have you heard ?   The priest's flown off.—
Up from hillocks, out of howes,

Swarm the demons and the Drows,
Black and ugly, big and little—
Ugh, how fierce they cut and cuff—!
Half my eye away they whittle ;
Half my soul they've carried off ;
With the stump I'll e'en make shift,
It will serve me well enough !

BRAND.

Girl, your thoughts are all adrift ;
See, I stand before you.

GERD.

You ?

Ay, but not the parson ?   Swift
From the peak my falcon flew,
Fiercely down the fells he hied him,
He was bitted and saddled too,
Through the nightfall blast he hiss'd,
And a man was set astride him,—
'Twas the parson, 'twas the priest !
Now the valley church is bare,
Lock and bar are bolted there ;
Ugly-church's day is past ;
M i n e shall get its due at last.
There the priest stands, tall and strong
Snowy surplice swathes his flank,
Woven of winter's drip and dank,
If you'd see him, come along ;
Parish-church is bare and blank ;
M y priest has so brave a song,
That the whole earth rings to hear it.

BRAND.

Who has bidden thee, shatter'd spirit,
Lure me with this idol-lay ?

GERD.

[*Coming into the garden.*]

Idols, idols?   What are they?
Oho!   That is what you mean:
Giant or pigmy, large or lean,
Always gilded, always gay.
Idols!   Look you where she stands!
See you 'neath her mantle stray
Baby-feet and baby-hands?
See you how those robes are gay,
That close-folded something keep
Like a little child asleep?
Back she shudders!   Hides her son!
Idols?—Man, I show you one!

AGNES.

Have you tears, Brand?   Can you pray?
Terror scorches mine away!

BRAND.

Woe's me, Agnes—I forbode
In her words the voice of God.

GERD.

Hark; now all the bells are loud,
Clanging down the savage fells!
See, what moving masses crowd
Upwards to those bidding bells!
See the thousand trolls uprisen
From the ocean-caves, their prison;
See the thousand dwarfs up-leaping
From the graves where they were sleeping
With the priest's seal on them set:
Grave and ocean cannot bind them,
Out they're swarming, chill and wet;—
Troll-babes that but shammed to die,

Grinning roll the rocks behind them:
" Mother, father ! " hark, they cry ;
Goodman, Goodwife, make reply ;
Then, as fathers among sons,
Move among their buried ones ;
Women lay their risen dead
At their bosoms to be fed,
Strutted scarce with prouder front
When they bore them to the font.
Life begins !   The parson's fled !

BRAND.

Get thee from me !   Direr still
Grows the vision——

GERD.

Hark, he's mocking !
He that sits by yon way-border,
Where it rears to scale the hill,
All their names as they go flocking
In his book he writes in order ;—
Ho ! he's wellnigh all the pack ;
For the parish-church is bare,
Lock and bar are bolted there,—
And parson's off on falcon-back !
  [*Leaps over the garden-fence and is lost in
  the moraine. Stillness.*

AGNES.

[*Approaches, and says in a low voice.*]
Late we linger : let us go.

BRAND.

[*Looking fixedly at her.*]
Shall our way be——
[*Points first to the garden-gate, then to the house-
  door.*]
   So ?—or so ?

AGNES.
[*Starts back shuddering.*]
Brand, your child,—your child !

BRAND.
[*Following her.*]
                                    Say rather :
Was I priest ere I was father ?

AGNES.
[*Drawing further back.*]
Though in thunder-crash it peal'd,
Unto that my lips are seal'd.

BRAND.
[*Following.*]
You are Mother : it is due
That the last word come from you.

AGNES.
I am Wife : I shall fulfil
All that you have heart to will.

BRAND.
[*Trying to grasp her arm.*]
Take the Cup of Choice from me !

AGNES.
[*Retreating behind the tree.*]
Mother then I should not be !

BRAND.
There a Judgment is let fall !

AGNES.

[*Vehemently.*]

Have you any choice at all !

BRAND.

Still the Judgment, gathering force !

AGNES.

Trust you wholly in God's Call ?

BRAND.

Yes !

[*Grasps her hand firmly.*]

And now 'tis yours to give

Final sentence : Die or live !

AGNES.

Go where God has fix'd your course　　　[*Pause.*

BRAND.

Late we linger : let us go.

AGNES.

[*Voiceless.*]

Shall our way be——— ?

BRAND.

[*Silent.*]

AGNES.

[*Pointing to the garden-gate.*]

So ?

BRAND.

[*Pointing to the house-door.*]

Nay,—so !

AGNES.

[Raising the child aloft in her arms.]

God ! The gift Thou canst require
I can lift it to thy sight !
Guide me through life's martyr-fire !

[Goes in.

BRAND.

*[Gazes a while before him, bursts into tears, clasps his
hands over his head, throws himself down on the
steps and cries:]*

Jesus, Jesus   give me light !

ACT FOURTH.

*Christmas Eve in the Manse. The room is dark.
Garden-door in the background; a window on
one side, a door on the other.* AGNES, *in mourning, stands at the window and gazes out into the
darkness.*

AGNES.

Still he comes not ! Comes not yet !—
Oh, how hard, with gloom beset,—
Still to wait and still to cry,—
Winning never a reply,—
Fast they fall, the softly sifted
Snowflakes ; in a shroud-like woof
They have swathed the old church roof———
[*Listens.*]
Hark ! the garden-latch is lifted !
Steps ! A man's step, firm and fast !
[*Hurries to the door and opens it.*]
Is it thou ? Come home ! At last !

BRAND *comes in, snowy, in travelling dress, which
he removes during what follows.*

AGNES
[*Throwing her arms about him.*]
Oh, how long thou wast away !
Go not from me, go not from me ;
All alone I cannot sway

The black clouds that overcome me;
What a night, what days have been
These two—and the night between!

BRAND.

I am with thee, child, once more.
[*He lights a single candle, which throws a pale
radiance over the room.*]
Thou art pale.

AGNES.

                    And worn and sad.
I have watch'd and long'd so sore;
And this little leafy bough—
Little, it was all I had,
Saved from summer until now
To bedeck our Christmas-tree,—
I have hung it there, Brand, see!
His the bush was, so we said;
Ah, 'twas his—it crown'd him dead!
                    [*Bursts into tears.*]
Look, from the snow it peers
Yonder, his—O God——

BRAND.

                    His grave.

AGNES.

O that word!

BRAND.

Have done with tears.

AGNES.

Yes—be patient—I'll be brave!
But my soul is bleeding still,
And the wound is raw and new—

Sapp'd is all my strength of will.
Oh, but better shall ensue !
Once these days are overworn,
Thou shalt never see me mourn !

BRAND.

Keep'st thou so God's holy Night?

AGNES.

Ah !   Too much thou must not crave !
Think—last year so sweet and bright,
This year carried from my sight ;
Carried—carried——

BRAND
[*Loudly.*]
                    To the grave !

AGNES.
[*Shrieks.*]
Name it not !

BRAND.
                    With lungs that crack,
Named it must be, if thou shrink—
Named, till echo rolls it back,
Like a billow from the brink.

AGNES.

Ah !   The word gives thee, too, pain.
How-so passionless thou boast thee !
On thy brow I see the stain
Of the agony it cost thee '

BRAND.

On my brow the drops that lie
Are but sea-spray from the storm.

AGNES.

And that dewdrop in thine eye,
Has it fallen from the sky?
No, ah! no, it is too warm,
'Tis thy heart's dew!

BRAND.

Agnes, wife,
Let us bravely face the strife;
Stand together, never flinch,
Struggle onward, inch by inch.
Oh, I felt a man out there!
Surges o'er the reef were dashing;
Horror of the storm-lit air
Still'd the sea-gull; hail was thrashing
Down upon the boiling sea.
In my skiff, that mid-fjord quiver'd,
Mast and tackle creak'd and shiver'd,
Tatter'd sails blew far a-lee,
Scarce a shred of them remaining,
Every nail and stanchion straining!
From the beetling summits sunder'd.
Down the avalanches thunder'd;
Stiff and stark, with corpse-like faces
Sat the rowers in their places.
Then the soul in me wax'd high;
From the helm I ruled them all,
Knowing well that One thereby
Had baptized me to His call!

AGNES.

In the tempest to be strong,
Eager in the stress of fight,
That is easy, that is light;
Think of me, who, all day long,
Still must croon without relief

The low swallow-song of grief;
Think of me, who have no charm
For the tedious pain of life;
Me, who, far from war's alarm,
Lack the fiery joys of strife:
Think, oh think, of me, who share **not**
Noble work, but brood and wait;
Me, who to remember dare not,
And who never can forget!

BRAND.

Thou no noble life-work!   Thou!
Never was it great as now.
Listen, Agnes; thou shalt know
What to me our loss has brought.
Oftentimes my light is low,
Dim my reason, dull my thought,
And there seems a kind of gladness
In immeasurable sadness.
Agnes—in such hours I see
God, as at no other, near;
Oh, so near, it seems to me
I could speak, and He would hear.
Like a lost child then I long
To be folded to his breast,
And be gather'd by His strong
Tender Father-arms to rest!

AGNES.

Brand, oh see Him so alway!
To thy supplication near—
God of love and not of fear!

BRAND.

No; I may not bar his way,
Nor run counter to my Call;

III   I

I must see Him vast, sublime
As the heavens,—a pigmy Time
Needs a giant God withal !
Oh, but thou mayst see Him near,
See Him as a Father dear,
Bow Thy head upon His breast,
There, when thou art weary, rest,
Then return, with face aglow
From His presence, fair and free,
Bear His glory down to me
Worn with battle-thrust and throe!
See, my Agnes ; so to share
Is the soul of wedded life :
His, the turmoil and the strife,
Hers the healing and the care;
This and this alone, the true
Wedlock, that makes one of two.
Since thou turnedst from the life
Of the world to be my wife,
Boldly cast thy lot with me,
This the work appointed thee
Mine the stir and stress of fight,
Battle in the burning sun,
Watching in the winter night ;
But for thee, when all is done,
To my parching lips to hold
Love's full wine-cup, and to fold
'Neath the breastplate's iron stress
The soft robe of tenderness.
Surely that work is not light !

AGNES.

Every work that I have sought
Is too hard for my weak skill ;
All the fibres of my will
Gather round a single thought.

Like a vision seems it still :
Let me have of tears my fill.
Help me so myself to see,—
What I am, and ought to be !
Brand,—last night, in stillest hush,
Open'd he my chamber door,
On his cheek a rosy flush,
And his little shirt he wore,—
Toddled so with childish tread
To the couch where I lay lonely,
" Mother ! " call'd to me, and spread
Both his arms, and smiled, but only
As if praying : " Make me warm."
Yea, I saw !—Oh, my heart bled———

BRAND.

Agnes !

AGNES.

Ah, his little form
Was a-cold, Brand ! Needs it must,
Pillow'd in the chilly dust.

BRAND.

That which lies beneath the sod
Is the corse ; the child's with God.

AGNES.

[*Shrinking from him.*]
Oh, canst thou without remorse
Thus our bleeding anguish tear ?
What thou sternly call'st the corse—
Ah, to me, my child is there !
Where is body, there is soul :
These apart I cannot keep,
Each is unto me the whole ;

Alf beneath the snow asleep
Is my very Alf in heaven!

BRAND.

Many a raw wound must be riven
Ere thy deep disease give way.

AGNES.

Yet have patience with me, pray,
Let me follow, not be driven.
Give me thy strong hand and guide me
Oh, and gently, gently chide me!
Thou whose voice in thunder-tones
Vibrates in the hour of strife,
For the soul that still with groans
Fights a fight for very life,
Hast thou no soft, piteous lay,
To beguile its pangs away?
Ne'er a message to uplift,
Point me to the dawn-fired rift?
God, as thou wouldst have me view Him,
Is a monarch on His throne.
How dare I, then, turn unto Him
With my lowly mother's moan?

BRAND.

Wouldst thou rather, haply, turn
To the God thou knew'st before?

AGNES.

Never, never, nevermore!
And yet oftentimes I yearn
Towards the daybreak, towards the light,
Towards the sunshine warm and golden.
Oh, the ancient saw is right:
" Lightly lifted, hardly holden "

All too vast this realm of thine,
Too gigantic to be mine.
Thou, thy word, thy work, thy goal,
Will austere, and steadfast soul,
Overhead the beetling height,
And the barrier fjord below,
Grief and memory, toil and night,
All vast,—were the Church but so !

BRAND.
[*Starting.*]
What ! the Church ?　　Again that thought ?
Is it bred an instinct blind
In the air ?

AGNES.
[*Shaking her head sadly.*]
Oh ask me not
To find reasons for my thought.
Instinct steals upon the sense
Like a perfume,—to and fro,
Blowing whither ?　　Blowing whence ?
I perceive it, that is all
And, unknowing, yet I know
That for me it is too small.

BRAND.
Truth may be from dreams divined.
In a hundred hearts I find
Self-begotten this one word ;
Even in hers, whose frantic call
From the mountain-side I heard :
" It is ugly, for 'tis small ! "
So she said ; and like the rest
Left her meaning half-express d.
Then of women came a score,

" Yes, it is too small," they cried;
They would have it spread and soar,
Like a palace in its pride.
Agnes—ah! I see it clear;
Thou the woman art whom God
Gave me for His angel-guide.
Safe alike from doubt and fear
Through the darkness thou hast trod,
Keeping still the even way,
Where I blindly went astray.
Thee no glamour captivated—
Once thy finger show'd the fated
Region where my life-work waited,
Check'd me, as I sought sublime,
To the vault of heaven to climb,
Turn'd my soaring glance within,
And that kingdom bade me win.
Now, a second time, thy word
Penetrates my soul like day,
Guides me where I vainly err'd,
Glorifies my weary way.
Small the Church is?   Be it so:
Then a greater Church shall grow.
Never, never did I wot
All God gave me, giving thee;
Now that cry of thine's for me:
Leave me not!   Oh leave me not!

AGNES.

All my sorrow I will quell,
I will dry the tears that well,
Seal in still sepulchral sleep
Memory's lone castle-keep;
Lay oblivion like a sea
Open between it and me,
I will blot the joyous gleams

From my little world of dreams,
Live, thy wife, alone for thee !

BRAND.

Steep the path is, high the goal.

AGNES.

Lead, nor sternly spur, my soul !

BRAND.

In a greater name I call.

AGNES.

One of whom thou saidst that still
He accepts the steadfast will,
Though the flesh be weak withal !   [*Going.*

BRAND.

Whither, Agnes ?

AGNES.
[*Smiles.*]
                Ah, to-day
Home must have its feast array
Thou my lavishness didst chide,
Mindest thou, last Christmastide ?
All the chamber flash'd with lights,
From the Christmas-tree there hung
Toys and wreaths and quaint delights;
There was laughter, there was song.
Brand, for us this year also
Shall the Christmas-candles glow,
Here shall all be deck'd and dight
For the great, still Feast to-night !
Here, if haply God should peep,
He of meek and lowly mind

Shall His stricken children find,
Babes, that humbly understand,
To have felt their Father's hand
Gives them not a right to weep.——
Seest thou now of tears a sign ?

BRAND.
[*Presses her to him a moment.*]
Child, make light : that work is thine.

AGNES.
[*Smiles sadly.*]
Thou thy greater Church shalt rear :
Oh—but end ere Spring is here !   [*Goes.*

BRAND.
Willing in her torments still,
Willing at the martyr's stake ;
Flesh may flag and spirit break,
But unbroken in her Will.
Lord, to her poor strength add Thine ;——
Be the cruel task not mine
At Thy bidding to unchain
Angry vultures of the Law,
Swift to swoop with ravening maw
And her heart's warm blood to drain !
I have strength to stand the strain.
Twofold agony let me bear,——
But be merciful to her !

A knock at the outer door.   THE MAYOR *enters.*

THE MAYOR.
A beaten man, I seek your door.

BRAND.

A beaten man ?

THE MAYOR.

As such I stand
Before you.　When I open'd war,
And sought to drive you from the land
The end I augur'd, I confess,
For you, was not just—well—success.

BRAND.

Indeed——?

THE MAYOR.

But though my cause I boast
The better, I'll contend no more.

BRAND.

And why ?

THE MAYOR.

Because you have the most.

BRAND.

Have I ?

THE MAYOR.

Oh, that you can't ignore :
Folks flock to you by sea and shore ;
And in the whole of my confine
A spirit has of late been rife,
Which, God's my witness, is not mine ;
Whence to conclude is only due,
That it originates with you.
Here is my hand : we'll end the strife !

BRAND.

War such as we wage does not cease,
Howe'er the vanquish'd cry " No more ! "

THE MAYOR.

Why, what should be the end of war
But reasonable terms of peace?
To kick at pricks is not my way,
I'm made of common human clay;
When at your breast the lance you feel
It is but reason to give place;—
With but a switch to parry steel,
'Tis just to make a volte-face;
Left of your cause the sole defender,
It is the wisest to surrender.

BRAND.

Two things are noticeable here.
First, that you call me strong.   Of men
I have the larger part.

THE MAYOR.

           That's clear.

BRAND.

Now, possibly: but when shall rise
The great dread day of sacrifice,
Who will have more supporters then?

THE MAYOR.

Of sacrifice?   Why, goodness me,
That's just the day we never see
At least, the sacrifice no worse is
Than drafts upon good people's purses;
The age is too humane to bring
Any more costly offering.
And what's most vexing is, that I
Myself have all along been noted
Of those who the Humane promoted

And hinder'd sacrifice thereby.
So that it may be fairly said,
I've put the axe to my own head,
Or, at the least, laid rods in store
To baffle all I've struggled for.

BRAND.

You may be right.　　But, furthermore
I hardly know how you can dare
Surrender your own cause as lost.
Be rods, or be they not, the cost,
Man's work is what he's fashion'd for,
And Paradise, for him, lies there.
'Twixt him and it though oceans swell,
And close at hand lie Satan's quarter,
May he for that cry " Toil, farewell—
The way to hell's distinctly shorter!" ?

THE MAYOR.

To that I answer : Yes and No.
Some final haven man must win ;—
If all our toil brings nothing in,
Who on a barren quest will go ?
The fact stands thus : we want reward
For every labour, light or hard ;
And if in arms we miss the prize,—
We gain our point by compromise.

BRAND.

But black will never turn to white !

THE MAYOR.

Respected friend, the gain is slight
Of saying : " White as yonder brae,"
When the mob's shouting : " Black as snow "

BRAND.

You join them, possibly ?

THE MAYOR.

Why, no—
I rather shout, not black, but gray,
The time's humane; asks apt compliance,
Not blunt and absolute defiance.
We stand on democratic ground,
Where what the people thinks is right;
Shall one against the mass propound
His special views on black and white ?
In short, you, having a majority,
Are best entitled to authority.
So I submit, as they submitted,
With you my humble lot I cast,
And may I by no soul be twitted
For not contending to the last !
Folks now consider, I perceive,
Petty and poor all I achieve ;
They say there's something of more worth
Than richer harvests wrung from earth ;
They are not willing as they were,
The necessary mite to spare ;
And the best cause, if will's not in it,—
There's very little hope to win it.
Believe me, 'tis no easy thing
To drop one's plans for roads and bridges,
For tapping meres and draining ridges,
And more besides that was in swing.
But, good Lord, what's a man to say ?
If he can't win, he must give way ;
Patiently trust that Time's his friend,
And to the blast astutely bend.
Now,—the folks' favour I've foregone

In just the way it first was won;
Ay, ay,—and by another track
I'll get my old possession back.

Brand.

So all your cunning, all your art,
Aim'd but to win the people's heart?

The Mayor.

God help me, no! The common good
And profit of this neighbourhood
Has been my single, sole desire.
But, I admit, there did conspire
The worker's hope of worthy hire
For day's work honestly pursued.
The fact stands thus: a resolute
And able man, with sense to hoot,
Demands to see his labour's fruit,
And not to drudge and sweat and groan
To profit an Idea alone.
With the best will I can't afford
To throw my interests overboard,
And give my brains without reward.
I've a large household to supply,
A wife, and of grown girls a store,
Who must be first provided for;—
Belly that's empty, throat that's dry,
The idea scarce will satisfy,
Where mouths so many must be fill'd.
And any man who should demur,
For him I have but one reply,—
He's an unworthy householder.

Brand.

And now your object is— ?

THE MAYOR.

To build.

BRAND.

To build?

THE MAYOR.

Why, yes,—the common state
To better, and my own to boot.
First I will build up the repute
I stood in till a recent date :—
The elections soon will be on foot :—
So I must set some scheme afloat,
Some booming enterprise promote ;
Thus I regain my lost authority,
And check the wane of my majority.
Now, I've reflected, to compete
With wind and tide wins no man's praises ;
The folk want " lifting," as the phrase is,
A work for which I'm all unmeet ;
I can but set them on their feet ;
Which can't be done unless they please,—
And here all are my enemies !
Whence I've resolved since such the case is,
After ripe thought, to find a basis
For making war with poverty.

BRAND.

You would uproot it ?

THE MAYOR.

No, not I !

It is a necessary ill
In every state : we must endure it ;
Yet may we, with a little skill,
In certain forms confine, secure it,
If only we begin in time.

He who would grow a bed of crime,
Let him with poverty manure it :
I'll set a dam to this manure !

BRAND.

How ?

THE MAYOR.

    Do you take me ?   I can cure
A want, of long and bitter proof,
By building, for the Town's behoof,
A Pest-house for the afflicted Poor.
Pest-house I call a thing projected
To rid us of the crime-infected.
And, I reflected, to the Pest-house
Might well be added an Arrest-house,
The cause with its effect confined
The selfsame bars and bolts behind,
And nothing but a wall between.
And, while my hand is in, I mean
In the same block to build withal
A wing for balls and ballotings,
Social and business gatherings,
With platform and Assembly-Hall ;
In short, a half-political,
Half-social, smart and festive Guest-house.

BRAND.

Sorely required ; this most of all ;
But yet there's one thing needed more.

THE MAYOR.

You mean a Mad-house ?   Yes, indeed ;
A very peremptory need ;
That was my own idea before.
But now, by friendly counsel wrought,
I've utterly renounced the thought ;

For who's to furnish the supplies
For such a giant enterprise?
To put a Mad-house up would come,
Believe me, to a pretty sum,
If all whom need and merit fitted,
Should be within its walls admitted.
We must not build for our caprice,
But note Time's current as it glides;—
The world moves on with giant strides,
Last year abundance, famine this;
You see to what a monstrous girth
The folks' necessities have swell'd,
Talents for everything on earth,
Headlong by seven-league boots propell'd,
Are swarming madly to the birth.
Thus it would be too dear a jest
To build posterity a nest
And let self, wife, and children go;
This tooth, I say, we can't afford:
Out with it therefore, by the Lord!

BRAND.

And then, there's the great Hall, you know,
For any madder than the rest.

THE MAYOR.
[*Delighted.*]

Yes, it would mostly be to spare!
Why, Brand, you've hit the nail-head there!
If fortunate our project's fate is,
We get to boot—a Mad-house gratis;
Here, shelter'd by the selfsame roof,
And by the selfsame flag defended,
All the essential strands are blended
That tinge and tone our social woof.

Here in one haven disembogues
The flood of Paupers and of Rogues;
With Lunatics who roam'd at large,
Subject to no man's check or charge;
Here too our Freedom's highest reach,
The election-strife, the storm of speech;
And here our Council-Hall, for framing
Measures to meet each public pest;
And here our Feast-Hall, for proclaiming
How well we'll guard the Past's bequest.
You see, then, if our Project stand,
The Cragsman has at his command
All he in reason can demand,——
The right to live as he thinks best.
God knows, how slender our resources,
But once our enterprise in force is,
I trust we may be with impunity
Styled a well-organised community.

BRAND.

But then the means—— ?

THE MAYOR.

　　　　　　　Ay, there's the knot,
As in all other things, in this.
Hardly to contributions wrought
Is Will, and if your help I miss,
I furl my flag without a thought:
But with your eloquent alliance
I'll bid all obstacles defiance,
And when all's done, your kind compliance,
Believe me, shall not be forgot.

BRAND.

In short, you'd buy me.

III　　　　　　　　　　　　　K

THE MAYOR.

For my aim
I should prefer another name :
I seek, with general good in view,
That gulf of difference to cross
Which you from me and me from you
Has sever'd, to our common loss.

BRAND.

In an ill-omen'd hour you came——

THE MAYOR.

Unfortunately yes, I own it :
Your recent loss,—I might have known it,
But your brave bearing re-assured me,
And need of public credit lured me.

BRAND.

In grievous or in gladsome season
I render help where need is plain ;
But, for another weighty reason,
This time your mission is in vain.

THE MAYOR.

And which, pray——?

BRAND.

I am building too.

THE MAYOR.

You building ? You adopt my view ?

BRAND.

Not altogether.
        [*Pointing out of the window.*]
            Do you see ?

THE MAYOR.

Yonder

BRAND.

Yes.

THE MAYOR.

That great ugly stall ?—
Why, that's the Parsonage granary.

BRAND.

No, not that ;—but the ugly, small——

THE MAYOR.

The Church ?

BRAND.

I mean to build it great.

THE MAYOR.

That, by the devil ! you shall not !
No man shall alter it one jot !
My plan 'twould utterly frustrate.
Mine's urgent, only waits the word,
By yours I'm absolutely floor'd ;
Two weapons can't at once be wielded,
Yield therefore— !

BRAND.

I have never yielded.

THE MAYOR.

You must, man, here.   Build my Arrest-house,
My Pest-house and my festive Guest-house,
Build all, the Mad-house comprehending,
And who'll ask, where the Church wants mending?
And why condemn it now to fall ?
'Twas well enough a while ago.

BRAND.

Possibly ; now it is too small.

THE MAYOR.

I never saw it full, I know.

BRAND

Even a single soul is scanted,
And has not room therein to soar

THE MAYOR.

[*Shaking his head in amazement.*]
(Which single soul but proves the more
How sorely my Asylum's wanted.)
       [*Changing his tone.*]
Let the Church be, is my advice.
One may regard it, in some wise,
As a rich heirloom of our age;
In fact, a noble heritage,
Which we not lightly may remove.
Nay, if my building project crashes,
I, like a Phoenix from the ashes,
Will live again in public love,
As one chivalrously intent
To save our ancient monument!
Here stood a heathen fane of old,—
'Twas in King Belë's reign, no doubt;
Then, later heroes more devout
Founded the Church with looted gold.
All-sacred in its antique dress,
Grand in its simple stateliness,
Till our own days it tower'd sublime——

BRAND.

But all these glories of old time
Lie long since buried deep in mould,
Of all surviving sign bereft.

THE MAYOR.

Just so !   They are so very old
That not a trace of them is left.
But in my late grandfather's day
A wall-hole still defied decay !

BRAND.

A wall-hole ?

THE MAYOR.

Fit to hold a tun !

BRAND.

But the wall's self ?

THE MAYOR.

          Oh, that was gone.
In plain terms then, I am compell'd
To say, your scheme is out of court :——
A barbarous and unparallel'd
Horrible sacrilege, in short.
And then the money,—do you dream
These folks are so profuse in spending,
That they'll contrive new cost by lending
Existence to a half-hatch'd scheme ?
When with a little deftness they
May so far patch the crumbling wall
That in our time it will not fall ?
But just go out !—the field survey,——
You'll find, I'm winner after all.

BRAND.

From no man will I wring a jot
To give my God house-harbourage :
With my own goods it shall be wrought;
In that one work my heritage

To the last penny shall be spent.——
Now, Mayor, are you still confident
That you can shake me from my thought?

THE MAYOR.
[*With folded hands.*]
I stand—as from the clouds dropp'd down
Such things are even in a Town
Scarce heard of,——and yet here, for us,
Who long to the necessitous
Have closed our purses and our doors,
You loose this flood of gifts unbounded
That ripples, flashes, foams and pours——.
—No, Brand, I'm utterly dumbfounded

BRAND.
In thought I long ago resign'd
My wealth———

THE MAYOR.
            Yes, whisper'd hints have flown
Pointing to something of the kind.
But I regarded them as wind.
How many men give all they own
Without a tangible return ?
However, that's your own concern.——
Go on ! I'll follow. You're in feather,
You can act freely, work and sway.——
Brand, we will build the Church together

BRAND.
What, you are willing to give way ?

THE MAYOR.
Dear God's my witness, that I am !
And shall be while my wits are sound !

When one would fatten, pamper, cram,—
Another milk and shear and flay,—
Where, think you, will the flock be found?
Death and destruction, I'm your man!
I'm fire and fury for the plan'
Thrill'd, agitated, nay, affected!
Providence prompted the design
That led me to your door to-night,
For sure, without the hint of mine,
Your plan had scarcely been projected,
Or, at the least, scarce seen the light!
And thus the Church, conceived aright,
Will by my means have been erected'

BRAND.

But, don't forget, we must lay low
That towering relic of the past'

THE MAYOR.
[*Looking out.*]

Seen in the twofold glimmer cast
By the new moon and the fresh snow,
It seems a sort of—rubbish-heap.

BRAND.

What, Mayor!

THE MAYOR.

    It is too old to keep!
I fail entirely to explain it,
Till now it never struck my eye,—
The weathercock stands all awry;
It would be monstrous to retain it.
And where are architecture, style,
Rightly regarded, in the pile?
What terms can give that arch its due?
An architect would call it vile;—

And really I must share his view.
And then that roof with moss-tufts blowing,—
Bless me, they're none of Belë's growing.
No, we may overmuch assert
The reverence for ancient glories !
One fact, at least, there's no o'erthrowing,
That this old rotten hut no more is
But just a very heap of dirt !

BRAND.

But if the people's voice should storm
At those who seek to lay it low—?

THE MAYOR.

I will it though they all cry No.
This Christmas with the least delay
I'll put the thing in proper form,
And launch it smoothly on its way.
I'll write, I'll agitate, I'll sway !
Ay, ay—you know the stuff I'm made of!
And if I cannot hire or hound
The foolish flock to help to end it,
With my own hands I'll rive and rend it,
Timber by timber, to the ground.
Nay, though I had to call the aid of
My wife and all my girls as well,
Down it should come, by death and hell

BRAND.

This language has another sound
Than that which earlier from you fell.

THE MAYOR.

To be humane is to repress
All manner of One-sidedness.
And sure, if truth the poet utters,
Precisely what is to be sought

In thinking is "the winged thought,"—
That is to say—the thought that flutters.
Farewell.

        [*Taking his hat.*]
    I have to see the band.

          BRAND.

The what ?

        THE MAYOR.

        Just think, within our land
This morning two of us laid hand
On a foul-favour'd gipsy-horde,
So I got help with rope and cord,
And now they're in your neighbour's ward
Next to the North, but—devil clip me !—
If just a couple didn't slip me———

          BRAND.

The bells are ringing : Peace to Men.

        THE MAYOR.

Why came this hell-brood hither, then ?
Yet in a sense, they are, 'tis true,
Kin to this parish,—
       [*Laughing.*]
           Nay to you.
Hark to a riddle ; read it right,
If you have power and appetite.
There be, who in effect derive
From her, by whom you are alive,
But owe their actual origin
To coming of another kin.

          BRAND.
      [*Shaking his head.*]
O God, so many riddles rise
Before our baffled, helpless eyes !

THE MAYOR.

But this one's very lightly guess'd.
You must have often, heretofore,
Heard tell one story or another
Of that poor fellow here by West
Whose head four parsons' learning bore;
He went a-wooing to your Mother.

BLAND.

What then?

THE MAYOR.

          Conceive,—a girl of gold
She sent him to the right-about
Promptly, as might have been foretold.
And how d'ye think he took the flout?
Half mad with grief he wander'd out,
Mated at last another bride,
A gipsy,—and, before he died,
Enrich'd with issue this foul band
That sins and starves about the land.
Nay, on this parish he conferr'd
One bastard imp—as souvenir
Of his illustrious career.

BRAND.

Namely—?

THE MAYOR.
The gipsy-urchin Gerd.

BRAND.
[*In muffled tones.*]

Ah—so!

THE MAYOR.
[*Gaily.*]
          Confess, the riddle's good!
His issue in effect derive

From her by whom you are alive;
For the first cause of all the brood
Was, that he loved and she withstood.

BRAND.

Advise me, Mayor; can you tell
Some means of giving them relief?

THE MAYOR.

Tut, clap them in a Bridewell cell.
They're overhead in debt to hell;
To save them were to play the thief
With Satan, who will lose his trade
If earth restore not what he made.

BRAND.

You plann'd to build a house, to better
This naked misery and dearth——

THE MAYOR.

That plan was, by its own begetter,
Slain in the moment of its birth.

BRAND.

If after all though—it were well——

THE MAYOR.
[*Smiling.*]

This language has another sound
Than that which earlier from you fell.
　　　[*Clapping him on the shoulder.*]
What's buried, leave it in the ground
Man must not dash his deed with doubt.
Farewell, farewell, I can't remain,
I must be off and scour the fell,
To seek this nest of truants out.
A merry Yule! We'll meet again!
My greetings to your wife. Farewell! [*Goes.*

BRAND.
[After a meditative silence.]
O expiation without end !——
So wildly mingle, strangely blend
The threads that human fortune spin,——
Sin tangled with the fruit of sin,
Pouring its own pollution in,——
That he who eyes their mazy flight
Sees foulest Wrong grow one with Right.
[Goes to the window, and after a long look out.]
My little child, lamb without stain,
Thou for my mother's deed wast slain ;
A shatter'd spirit bore His voice
Whose throne the crested heavens sustain,
And bade me cast the die of choice.
And this distracted soul had birth
Because my mother's clave to earth.
Thus the Lord, sowing fruit of crime,
Reaps retribution in His time,
And, reaching down from His high dome,
Strikes the third generation home.
[Starts back in horror from the window.]
Yes, God is above all things just,
And retribution is His goal ;
Only by sacrifice the soul
Achieves redemption from the dust ;
Hard truth, our age appall'd descries,
And, therefore, stubbornly denies.
[Walks up and down the room.]
To pray ?   Ah, pray—a word that slips
Easily over all men's lips ;
A coin by all men lightly paid.
What's prayer ?   In storm and stress to shout
Unto the vague Unknown for aid.
Upon Christ's shoulders beg a place,

And stretch both hands to Heaven for grace—
While knee-deep in the slough of doubt.
Ha ! if there needed nothing more
I might like others dare to raise
My hand and batter at His door
Who still is " terrible in praise."—
　　　　　[*Pauses and reflects.*]
And yet in uttermost despair,
In shuddering sorrow's deepest deep,
When Alf at last had sunk to sleep,
And all his mother's kisses vain
Won not the lost smile back again—
What felt I—if it was not prayer ?
Whence came that trance, that ecstasy,
That rushing music, like a blast,
That sang afar and hurried past,
Bore me aloft and set me free ?
Was it the ecstasy of prayer ?
Did I with God hold converse there ?
My anguish—did it reach his ears ?
Did he look down and see my tears ?
I know not.　　Barr'd is now the door,
The darkness deeper than before,
And nowhere, nowhere any light !
Yes, She—who, darkling, yet hath sight—
　　　　　[*Calls in anguish.*]
Light, Agnes—light, if light thou hast !

Agnes opens the door and enters with the lighted
　　Christmas candles ; a bright glow falls over the
　　room.

　　　　　　BRAND.

Light !

　　　　　　AGNES.

See, the Yule light, Brand, at last !

BRAND.
[*Softly.*]

The Yule light !   Ha !

AGNES.
[*Putting them on the table.*]
                              Have I been slow ?

BRAND.

No, no.

AGNES.

Thou must be cold, Brand !

BRAND.
[*Loudly.*]
                                                No

AGNES.
[*Smiling, fills the stove.*]

How stern !   It is thy pride of will,
That scorns the darkness and the chill.

BRAND.
[*Walking up and down.*]

H'm, Will !

AGNES.
[*To herself as she decks the room.*]
            Here must the candles stand.
Last year he stretch'd his tiny hand
After the glancing, dancing light :
He was so joyous and so bright ;
He started from his little chair,
And ask'd me if a sun it were.
            [*Moves the candles a little.*]
See ! now the candle's glow falls—there !

Now from his bed my boy can see
The window gleaming cheerily;
Now can he peer out of the gloom
Silently into our lit room—
But, ah! the glass is dim; stay, stay—
I'll wipe the dew of tears away
And make it smile——   [*Dries the pane.*

BRAND.
[*Softly as he watches her.*]
                          When in this breast
Will the wild waters sink to rest?
To rest they must!

AGNES.
[*To herself.*]
                          How bright the glow
It seems as though the sundering wall
Had sunk; the low room grown a hall,
The murky world of ice and snow
Sudden become a shelter'd nest,
Where cosily my child may rest.

BRAND.
What dost thou, Agnes?

AGNES.
[*To herself.*]
                          Peace, I pray!

BRAND.
[*Nearer.*]
Why didst thou ope the curtain?

AGNES.
                                    Nay,
I dreamt, and knew not what I did!

BRAND.

Snares in that dream of thine lie hid ;
Close it again.

AGNES.

[*Pleading.*]
Brand !

BRAND.

Close, I say !

AGNES.

Oh, be not harsh, it is not right.

BRAND.

Close, close !

AGNES.

[*Drawing it.*]
Now all is close and tight ;
Yet in my heart I scarce can deem
God injured if, at sorest need,
In the brief respite of a dream
I tasted comfort.

BRAND.

No, indeed !
He is a feeling Judge and kind,
And will indulgently forbear,
If in thy service He should find
Some idol-worship here and there.

AGNES.

[*Bursts into tears.*]
Oh, say, when will He cease to crave ?
My wings are weak—I faint and fall———

BRAND.

He gives to the devouring wave
Who in his giving gives not all.

AGNES.

I have given all ; I have no more.

BRAND.
[*Shakes his head.*]
Yet other gifts remain behind.

AGNES.
[*Smiling.*]
Ask : I've the courage of the poor!

BRAND.

Give!

AGNES.

Take ! Ah, Brand, thou'lt nothing find

BRAND.

Thy memories and thy moans thou hast,
Thy longings and thy sinful sighs————

AGNES.
[*Despairingly.*]
I have my heart of agonies !
Tear, tear it from me !

BRAND.
Thou hast cast
Thy offerings in the yawning deep
For nothing, if thou count them losses.

III　　　　　　　　　　　　　　　　L

AGNES.

[*Shudders.*]

Narrow is thy Lord's way, and steep.

BRAND.

That way Will cannot choose but keep.

AGNES.

And Mercy's is——

BRAND.

[*Peremptorily.*]

Beset with crosses.

AGNES.

[*Gazes before her ; then, trembling.*]

Now manifest and open lies,
Abysmal as the depths of space,
That mystic Word.

BRAND.

What word ?

AGNES.

He dies

Who sees Jehovah face to face.

BRAND.

[*Throws his arms about her and clasps her close.*]

O look not on Him !   Close thine eyes !
Hide thee, O hide thee !

AGNES.

Must I ?

BRAND.

[*Lets her go.*]

No.

AGNES.

Thou sufferest, Brand.

BRAND.

Thou art so dear.

AGNES.

Thou lov'st me, but thy love I fear.
'Tis stern.

BRAND.

Too stern ?

AGNES.

Ask not ; whereso
Thou goest, I will also go !

BRAND.

Think'st thou without design I won thee
Out of thy gladsome gay content,
Or, half in earnest, laid upon thee
The call to self-abandonment ?
Woe to us both ; too dear we paid,
Too vast a sacrifice we made ;
Thou art my wife : I crave thee all
To live according to our call.

AGNES.

Crave ; only leave me not.

BRAND.

Indeed
I must; for rest and peace I need.
Soon shall the great new Church arise !

AGNES.

My little Church a ruin lies.

BRAND.

It was a blessed wind that blew
And thy heart's idol overthrew !
       [Clasps her as if in dread.]
Peace be upon thee—and, through thee,
Peace also upon mine and me !
       [Goes towards the side-door.

AGNES.

Brand, may I softly set ajar
One hateful window-barrier,—so ?
Only a little ?   May I ?

BRAND.
[In the doorway.]
      No.
      [Goes into his room.

AGNES.

Closed, all closed with bolt and bar !
Seals on every passion set !
Seal'd to sorrow and to sigh,
Seal'd the grave and seal'd the sky,
Seal'd to feel—and to forget !
I will out !   I gasp for breath
In this lonely house of death.
Out ?   Oh, whither ?   Angry eyes
Glare upon me from the skies !
Can I, flying, high or low,
Bear my treasure where I go ?
Can I from my breast unsphere
The mute vacancy of fear ?—
      [Listens at BRAND's *door.]*
Loud he reads, he cannot hear.
There's no comfort !   There's no way
God is busy ; lists to-day

But to song and praise and blessing
Of the happy, child-possessing,
Richly-gifted of the earth.
Christmas is the feast of mirth.
Me He sees not, nor takes heed
Of a lonely mother's need.—
> [*Goes cautiously to the window.*]

Shall I draw the curtain back,
Till the clear and kindly ray
Chase the horror of night away
From his chamber bare and black?
Nay, he is not there at all.
Yule's the children's festival,
He hath got him leave to rise,
Haply now he stands, and cries,
Stretches little arms in vain
To his mother's darken'd pane.
Was not that a baby's voice?
Alf, I've neither will nor choice!
All is barr'd and bolted here.
'Tis thy father's bidding, dear!
Alf, I may not open now!
An obedient child art thou!
We ne'er grieved him, thou and I.
Oh, fly home then to the sky,
There is gladness, there is light,
There thy merry comrades stay
Till thou come to join their play.
Oh, but weep not in their sight,
Nor to any soul betray
That thy father bade me lock,
When thy little hand did knock.
Years bring sterner, sadder stress
Than a little child may guess.
Say, he sorrow'd, say, he sigh'd;
Say, he wove the garden's pride

All into a wreath for thee.
'Tis his doing! Canst thou see?
    [*Listens, starts, and shakes her head.*]
Oh, I dream! Not bar and wall
Only from my love divide me.
When the purging fire hath tried me
In its anguish, then alone
Shall the parting barriers fall
And the mighty bolts be batter'd,
And the vaulted dungeons shatter'd,
And the prison hinges groan!
Much, oh, much is to be done
Ere we parted twain be one.
I with silent, toiling hands
Still will labour on, to fill
The abyss of his commands;
I shall nerve me, I shall will.
But it is the Feast this eve—
Last year's how unlike! And wait
We will honour it in state.
I will fetch my treasures forth,
Whereof the uncounted worth
Best a mother can conceive,
To whose spirit they express
All her life-lost happiness.
    [*She kneels down by the cupboard, and takes*
      various things out of a drawer. At the
      same moment, BRAND *opens the door, and*
      is about to speak, when he observes her
      occupation, checks himself and remains
      standing. AGNES *does not see him.*

BRAND.
[*Softly.*]
Haunting still the mortal mound,
Playing in Death's garden-ground.

AGNES.

Lo, the robe, the veil that clad
At the font my little lad.
Under it his cloak I've laid—
    [*Holds it up, gazes at it, and laughs.*]
Lord, how brave it looks and bright!
Ah, he was a bonny sight
In his festal robes array'd!
Here's the scarf, the cape he wore
When the keen wind first he bore;
Longer was it than was meet
Then, but quickly grew too spare—
I will lay it with them there.
Gloves and stockings—(Oh, what feet!)
And his hood of silken fold
That had fenced him from the cold,
All unused and clean and sweet.
Oh, and there the wrappings warm
That should shield his little form
For the journey, from the storm
When again I laid them by,
Weary unto death was I!

BRAND.

    [*Clasps his hands in anguish.*]
Mercy, God!   I strive in vain!
Shatter her last idol-shrine
By some other hand than mine!

AGNES.

Did I weep?   Behold, a stain!
Oh, my treasure!   Jewell'd prize,
Bath'd in floods from aching eyes,
Lit with fires of tortured Will,
Holy Crowning-vesture, worn

By a child to Death's font borne,
Oh, what riches have I still !

A sharp knock at the outer door ; AGNES *turns with a
    cry, and at the same moment sees* BRAND. *The
    door is burst open, and a* WOMAN, *raggedly
    dressed, enters hastily, with a child in her arms.*

THE WOMAN.
[*Looking at the child's clothes, calls to* AGNES.]
Thou rich mother, share with me !

AGNES.
Thou art richer far !

THE WOMAN.
                    I see,
Thou art of the common breed,
Cramm'd with words, and void of deed.

BRAND.
        [*Approaching her.*]
Tell me what thou seekest.

THE WOMAN.
                            Thee,
Troth, I do not seek, at least !
Rather to the wind and rain
Will I hurry out again,
Than be sermon'd by a priest ;
Rather to the wild sea fly,
Drown and rot beneath the sky,
Than I'll hear the black man tell
How I'm on my way to hell ;
Can I help—the devil take me—
Being what God chose to make me ?

BRAND.

[To himself.]

Voice and feature pierce me still
With a dim and icy dread.

AGNES.

Thou shalt warm thee, if thou'rt chill ;
And thy hungry child be fed.

THE WOMAN.

Where there's warmth and where there's light
Brats of gipsies may not stay ;
We must haunt the lone highway,
Hill and forest, heath and height ;
We must wander, we must roam,
Leave to others house and home.
I must swiftly from this place.
Dogs of justice are behind me,
Mayor, bailiff, all in chase,
Hungering to catch and bind me !

BRAND.

Here thou shalt have shelter.

THE WOMAN.

Here !

Roof'd above and wall'd about ?
No ! The winter night is clear,
And the breezes blithe without.
But a rag to wrap the child !
That were something ! Sooth, its wild
Rascal brother fled, and bore
With him all the clouts it wore.
Look, it lies half naked—blue,
Stiff and stark and frozen through,
By the storm-wind's icy breath.

BRAND.

Woman, on the road to death,
Free thy infant from thy doom ;
Free him from thy grief and gloom
Of his birth I'll blot the brand.

THE WOMAN.

Much, sooth, thou dost understand !
Such a wonder none on earth
Can, nor shall do, though he can !
War on you that set the ban,—
Wot ye where it was, that birth ?
In a ditch-side, on the ground,
Gamblers drank and shouted round—
Christen'd in the sleety slime,
Cross'd with charcoal-ashes' grime,
Suckled with a spirit-flask ;—
When his mother bore him first
There were some stood by and cursed,
Who could they be, do you ask ?
Bless you !   Why, the baby's father,
Or,—the baby's fathers rather !

BRAND.

Agnes ?

AGNES.

Yes.

BRAND.

Thy duty's clear.

AGNES.

[Shuddering.]

Never ! never ! Brand, to her !

THE WOMAN.

Give me, give me !   Give me all !

Silk and broider'd jacket small!
Nought's too good, and nought too bad,
If 'twill warm my starving lad.
He'll be going by-and-by.
Thaw his body ere he die !

BRAND.
[*To* AGNES.]
Choice is calling !   Hear'st thou now ?

THE WOMAN.
Store enough of clothes hast thou
For thy dead child : hast thou none
For my death-doom'd living one ?

BRAND.
Is not this a warning cry
Importuning bodefully ?

THE WOMAN.
Give !

AGNES.
'Tis sacrilege blood-red
Desecration of the dead !

BRAND.
Vainly given to death he was
If thou at the threshold pause.

AGNES.
[*Crushed.*]
I obey.   My heart's quick root
I will trample under foot.
Woman, come thou and receive,
I will share it with thee.

THE WOMAN.

Give !

BRAND.

Share it, say'st thou ?—Agnes ; share it ?

AGNES.

[*Wildly.*]

I will rather die than spare it
All !   See, inch by inch I've bent
To thy will ; my force is spent !
Half's enough ; she needs no more !

BRAND.

Was the whole too much before,
When for thy child it was meant ?

AGNES.

[*Gives.*]

Woman, take ; in this was clad |
At the font my little lad.
Here the scarf, cloak, mantle, good
For the night-air, here the hood
Warm for winter ; take this last——

THE WOMAN.

Give me !

BRAND.

Is this all thou hast ?

AGNES.

[*Gives again.*]

Take the crowning vesture worn,
By the child to Death's Font

THE WOMAN.

So ! I see there's nothing more.
I'll clear out without delay,
Dress my baby at the door—
Then with all my pack away !   [*Goes.*

AGNES.

[*In violent inner conflict ; at length asks.*]
Is it reason, Brand, to lay
Further bidding on me ?

BRAND.

         Say,
Didst thou with a glad heart go
To thy task of giving ?

AGNES.

         No.

BRAND.

Then thy gift is vainly will'd
And His bidding unfulfill'd.   [*Going.*

AGNES.

[*Remains silent until he is near the door, then calls.*]
Brand !

BRAND.
What wilt thou ?

AGNES.

         I have lied—
See, I'm humbled, I am grieved.
Never knew'st thou nor believed,
Anything was left beside.

BRAND.

Well ?

AGNES.

[*Takes a folded child's cap from her bosom.*]
          See, one I thought to hide—
One !

BRAND.

     The cap ?

AGNES.

               Yes, tear-bewet,
Clammy with his mortal sweat,
There in my beating bosom set !

BRAND.

In thy idol-bonds abide.   [*Going.*

AGNES.

Hold !

BRAND.

     What wilt thou ?

AGNES.

               Thou dost know.
          [*Holds out the cap to him*

BRAND.

[*Approaches and asks, without taking it.*]
Gladly given ?

AGNES.
Gladly !

BRAND.

               So.
At the door she lingers yet.   [*Goes.*

AGNES.

Shiver'd, shatter'd—pluck'd away—
All that bound me to the clay.

[*Stands a while motionless ; by degrees her
face assumes an expression of radiant
gladness.* BRAND *returns ; she flies joyously towards him, flings herself about his
neck, and cries.*]

I am free, Brand, I am free!

BRAND.

Agnes!

AGNES.

     Night is fled from me!
All the terrors that oppress'd
Like an incubus my breast,
In the gulf are sunk to rest!
Will hath conquer'd in the fray,
Cloud and mist are swept away ;
Through the night, athwart the Dead,
Streaks of morning glimmer red.
Graveyard !   Graveyard !   By the word
Now no more a tear is stirr'd ;
By the name no wound is riven,
Risen is the child to heaven !

BRAND.

Agnes !   Thou hast conquered now

AGNES.

I indeed have conquer'd.   Yes ;
Conquer'd death and bitterness !
Oh, look up, look heavenward, thou
See, before the throne he stands—
As in old days—radiant, glad,

To us stretching down his hands!
Though a thousand mouths I had,
Leave to ask, and to obtain,
Never one of them should pray
For his coming back again.
O how wond'rous is God's way!
By that sacrifice, so grievous,
Won from bondage is my soul;
He was given us but to leave us,
Died to lure me to the goal.
Thanks be to thee that thy hand
Stoutly strove and firmly led—
Ah, I saw thine own heart bled.
Now it is for thee, instead,
In the vale of choice to stand,
Now for thee to hear the call
Of the awful Nought or All.

BRAND.

Agnes, this is darkly said;—
Vanquish'd, lo, our sorrow lies!

AGNES.

Thou forget'st the word of dread:
Whoso sees Jehovah dies!

BRAND.

[*Starts back.*]
Woe upon me! What a light
Thou has kindled! Never! No!
I have stalwart hands for fight,
And I will not let thee go!
Tear all earthly ties from me,
All possessions I will lose,
Only never, never thee!

AGNES.

At the cross-way stand'st thou : choose
Quench the kindled light I brought,
Fence the fountain of my thought,
Give me back my idol treasures
(Still she lingers by the door),
Give me back the earthly pleasures
Of the bright, blind days of yore ;
Thrust me back into the pit
Where till now I lulled my sin,
Deeper, deeper thrust me in—
Thou canst lightly compass it ;
Clip my wings and check my flight,
Load my feet, and drag me bound
Down, down from thy dizzy height
To my lowly native ground ;
Let me lead the life I led
When the darkness yet was dread :
If thou darest thus to lose,
Then, as ever, I am thine ;
At the cross-way stand'st thou : choose !

BRAND.

Woe, if such a choice were mine.
Ah, but in some place afar,
Where no bitter memories are,
Death and darkness thou shalt brave !

AGNES.

Hast thou here thy work forgotten,
Holy work—and holy grave ?
And the thousands sin-besotten,
It is here thy task to save—
Those thou guidest for God's sake
To the Fountain that renews ?
At the cross-way stand'st thou ; choose

BRAND.

Then I have no choice to make.

AGNES.

[*Throws herself on his neck.*]
Thanks for that, and thanks for all !
Thou the weary one hast led ;
Over me the dank mists fall,
Thou wilt watch beside my bed.

BRAND.

Sleep ! thy day's work now is done.

AGNES.

Done, and now the lamp alight.
I have fought out all my night,
I am weary of the sun.
Oh, but praising God is best !
Brand, good-night !

BRAND.

      Good-night !

AGNES.

                      Good-night
Thanks for all.   Now I will rest.

                          [*Goes*

BRAND.

[*Clenches his hands against his breast.*]
Soul, be patient in thy pain !
Triumph in its bitter cost.
All to lose was all to gain ;
Nought abideth but the Lost !

ACT FIFTH.

A year and a half later. The new Church stands complete, and adorned for consecration. The river runs close beside it. A misty morning, early.

The SEXTON *is busy hanging garlands outside the Church; shortly after comes the* SCHOOLMASTER.

THE SCHOOLMASTER.

At work already?

THE SEXTON.

               None too soon.
Lend me a hand; I must festoon
The path, to keep the march in trim.

THE SCHOOLMASTER.

Before the Manse I see ascending
Something that rears a rounded rim—

THE SEXTON.

Ay, surely, surely!

THE SCHOOLMASTER.

               What is pending?

THE SEXTON.

Why, it is what they call a shield
With Parson's name in a gold field

THE SCHOOLMASTER.
To-day the valley's in high feather.
From far and wide they're flocking hither,
The fjord with sails is all agleam.

THE SEXTON.
Yes; they've awaken'd from their dream.
In the late Pastor's day, no breast
With bitterness and strife was cumber'd,
Each slumber'd as his neighbour slumber'd,
—I'm not quite certain which is best.

THE SCHOOLMASTER.
Life, Sexton, life!

THE SEXTON.
         Yet you and I
Pass this "life" unregarding by;
How comes it?

THE SCHOOLMASTER.
         Why, before, the folk
Slumber'd, and nowise toil'd, as we did;
We fell asleep when they awoke,
Because we were no longer needed.

THE SEXTON.
But yet you said that life was best?

THE SCHOOLMASTER.
By Dean and deacon that's profess'd.
And I too say so, like the rest,—
Provided, mind, the "life" in view
Is that of the great Residue.
But we two serve another law
Than that which holds the mass in awe;

Set by the State to guard and guide,—
Look, we must stand against the tide,
Cherish the Church and Education,
And keep aloof from agitation.
Briefly, in nothing take a side.

THE SEXTON.

But Parson's in it, heart and soul.

THE SCHOOLMASTER.

And just in that forgets his rôle.
His own superiors, well I know,
Look with displeasure on his action,
And, dared they but offend his faction,
Had thrown him over long ago.
But he is fine; he smells a rat;
He's got a recipe for that.
He builds the Church.   Here you may glue
All eyes up, if you will but do.
What's done none has a thought to spare for;
The doing of it's all they care for.
So they who follow, and we who lead,
All equally are men of deed.

THE SEXTON.

Well, you have sat in the great Thing,
And ought to know the Land and Folk;
But one who travell'd through the glen
A little after we awoke
Said, we'd been sleeping folks till then,
But, having waked,—were promising.

THE SCHOOLMASTER.

Yes; we're a promising folk, of course,—
And mighty promises we're giving,—

So fast we stride, we'll soon be living
Elucidations of their force.

The Sexton.

One thing I've ponder'd many a day;
You've studied,—what do folks intend
By that same " People's Promise," pray ?

The Schoolmaster.

A People's Promise, my good friend ?
That were a long investigation ;
But 'tis a thing that is pursued
By force of sheer anticipation ;
A grand Idea they must make good
In future, be it understood.

The Sexton.

Thanks ; I see that at any rate ;
But there's another point I'd fain
Beg of you briefly to explain.

The Schoolmaster.

Speak freely.

The Sexton.

    Tell me, at what date
Comes, what is call'd the future ?

The Schoolmaster.

               Why,
It never does come !

The Sexton.

       Never

The Schoolmaster.

             No,
And only follows Nature so.

For when it comes, you see, 'tis grown
The Present, and the Future's flown.

THE SEXTON.

Why, yes, to that there's no reply;
That logic one must needs accept.
But—when then is the promise kept?

THE SCHOOLMASTER.

A Promise is a future-dated
Pact, as I have already stated;
'Tis kept in Future.

THE SEXTON.

     That is clear.
When will the Future, though, be here!

THE SCHOOLMASTER.
[*Aside.*]

You blessed Sexton!
[*Aloud.*]

     Worthy friend,
Must I the argument recall?
The Future cannot come at all,
Because its coming is its end.

THE SEXTON

Thank you.
THE SCHOOLMASTER.

    In all conceptions lies
Something that looks like artifice,
But yet is quite direct and plain,—
That is to say, for any brain
Able to reckon up to ten.
To make a promise means, at last,
To break it, spite of best intent;

Truth to one's word has always pass'd
For hard ; but you may just as well
Prove it purely impossible,—
If you've an eye for argument.—
There, let this Promise-question be !
Come tell me———— !

THE SEXTON.
Hist !

THE SCHOOLMASTER.
What is it ?

THE SEXTON.
Hark

THE SCHOOLMASTER.
I hear the organ play !

THE SEXTON.
'Tis he.

THE SCHOOLMASTER.
The Pastor ?

THE SEXTON.
Even so.

THE SCHOOLMASTER.
Save the mark
But he is out betimes !

THE SEXTON.
I guess
He stirr'd no pillow yesternight.

THE SCHOOLMASTER.
What do you say ?

THE SEXTON.

All is not right.
He's felt the pang of loneliness
Since first his widowhood began.
He hides his sorrow all he can ;
But, whiles, it may not be controll'd;
His heart's a jar that will not hold,
And overflows by base and brim ;—
So then he plays. 'Tis like a wild
Weeping for buried wife and child.

THE SCHOOLMASTER.

It is as if they talk'd with him——

THE SEXTON.

As if one suffer'd, one consoled——

THE SCHOOLMASTER.

H'm—if one dared to be affected !

THE SEXTON.

Ah,—if one did not serve the State

THE SCHOOLMASTER.

Ah,—if one bore no leaden weight
Of forms that have to be respected

THE SEXTON.

Ah,—if one dared toss tape and seal
And ledger to the deuce for ever !

THE SCHOOLMASTER.

And leave off striving to be clever ;
And, Sexton, if one dared to feel !

THE SEXTON.

No one is near,—let's feel, my friend !

THE SCHOOLMASTER.

We cannot fitly condescend
To smirch ourselves in human slime.
Let no man, says the Parson, dare
To be two things at the same time ;
And, with the best will, no one can
Be an official and a man ;
Our part in all things is, to swear
By our great exemplar—the Mayor.

THE SEXTON.

Why just by him ?

THE SCHOOLMASTER.

            Do you recall
The fire that wreck'd his house, and yet
The deeds were rescued, one and all ?

THE SEXTON.

It was an evening——

THE SCHOOLMASTER.

            Wild and wet,
And like ten toiling men toiled he ;
But indoors stood the Devil in glee
Guffawing, and his wife shriek'd out :
" O save your soul, sweet husband !　See,
Satan will have you ! "　Then a shout
Rang backward through the surging vapours :
" My soul may go to hell for me ;
Just lend a hand to save the papers ! "
Look, that's a Mayor—without, within !
From top to toe, from core to skin ;
He'll win his way, I'm certain, yonder,
Where his life's toil shall have its price.

THE SEXTON.

And where may that be ?

THE SCHOOLMASTER.

      Where, I wonder,
But in the good Mayors' Paradise.

THE SEXTON.

My learned friend !

THE SCHOOLMASTER.
    What now ?

THE SEXTON.

       A token
Of our fermenting age I hear,
Methinks, in every word you've spoken ;
For that it does ferment is clear.
Witness the reverence all refuse
To old-established Wont and Use.

THE SCHOOLMASTER.

What moulders, in the mould's its doom,
What rots must nourish what is fresh ;
Their vitals canker and consume,
Let them cough up the imposthume,
Or to the grave with their dead flesh !
There's ferment, yes ; past fear or hope,
That's plain without a telescope.
The day our ancient Church lay low,
Everything with it seem'd to go
Wherein our life struck root and found
Its home-soil and its native-ground.

THE SEXTON.

Then on the throng a stillness came.

"Down with it!   Down with it!" they cried
At first; but soon that clamour died,
And many felt their ears a-flame,
And stole shy glances of distrust,
When the ancestral House of Prayer
Was to be levell'd—then and there,—
By hands unhallow'd, in the dust.

THE SCHOOLMASTER.

But countless bonds, they fancied, knit
Them ever to the ghost of it,
So long as yonder Palace lack'd
The final seal of consecration;
And so in anguish'd expectation
They watch'd it growing into fact,
And blinked before the glorious End,
When the old tatter should descend
And the new colours flaunt the gale.
But ever as the spire upclomb
They grew more silent and more pale,
And now,—well, now the End is come.

THE SEXTON.

Look at the throng.   Both young and old
Swarm hither.

THE SCHOOLMASTER.

          And by thousands told.—
How still they are!

THE SEXTON.

          And yet they moan,
Like sea fore-feeling tempest's fret.

THE SCHOOLMASTER.

It is the People's hearts that groan,

As if, with piercing doubts beset,
The great new age they did forebode,
Or were in solemn sessions met
To nominate another God.
Where, where's the priest,—I stifle here.
Would heaven that I could disappear !

THE SEXTON.

I too, I too !

THE SCHOOLMASTER.

In hours like this
No man well knows how deep he is.
Each depth a deeper depth revealing,
We will, then will not, and then doubt——

THE SEXTON.

My friend !

THE SCHOOLMASTER.
My friend !

THE SEXTON.
H'm !

THE SCHOOLMASTER.
Speak it out !

THE SEXTON.
I think, in very truth, we're feeling !

THE SCHOOLMASTER.
Feeling ?　Not I !

THE SEXTON.
Nor I, take warning !
A single witness I defy !

THE SCHOOLMASTER.

We're men, not school-girls, you and I.
My youngsters wait for me.   Good-morning.

[*Goes.*

THE SEXTON.

Just now I'd visions like a fool :
Now I'm again collected, cool,
And close as clasps !   To work I'll press !
Here's no more scope for hand or tool,
And Satan's couch is idleness.

[*Goes out at the other side.*

*The organ, which during what precedes has been
heard in an undertone, suddenly peals forth, and
ends with a discordant shriek. Shortly afterwards*
BRAND *comes out.*

BRAND.

No, I vainly, vainly seek
To unlock the heart of sound ;
All the song becomes a shriek.
Walls and arches, vault and ground,
Seem to stoop and crowd and throng,
Seem to clasp with iron force,
Seem to close around the song,
As the coffin round the corse!
Vain my effort, vain my suit,
All the organ's music's mute,
Fain a prayer I would have spoken,
But my lifted voice fell broken,—
Like the muffled moan it fell
Of a riven and rusted bell.
'Twas as if the Lord were seated
In the chancel, and beheld,
And in wrath, while I entreated,

All my piteous prayer repell'd !—
   Great shall be the House of God;
In my confidence I swore it;
Fearless, smote and wreck'd and tore it,
Swept it level with the sod.
Now the finish'd work stands fast.
As the people throng before it,
Still they cry : "How vast ! how vast ! "
Is it they see true or I,
Who no vastness can descry ?
Is it great ? The thing I will'd,
Is it in this House fulfill'd ?
Can the rushing fire of passion
That begot it, here be still'd ?
Was the Temple of this fashion
That I dream'd should overspan
All the misery of Man ?
   Ah, had Agnes stay'd with me,
Not thus vainly had I striven !
Small things greatly she could see,
From doubt's anguish set me free,
Clasp together Earth and Heaven
Like the green roof of the tree.
     [*He observes the preparations for the festival.*]
All with wreaths and banners hung;
Children practising their song;
So the Manse they surge and throng,—
Festal greetings they would bring me ;—
Yonder gleams my name in gold !—
Give me light, O God, or fling me
Fathom-deep beneath this mould !
In an hour begins the Feast
Every thought and every tongue
Will be ringing with " the priest
All their thoughts I can discern ;
All their words I feel them burn ;

All their praise, on elf-wings sped,
Rives me like an icy blast!
Oh, to be enfolded fast
In oblivion, hide my head
In a wild beast's hole at last!

THE MAYOR.

[*Enters in full uniform, radiant with
satisfaction, and greets him.*]

Here is the great day come at last,
The Sabbath to the toiling six;
Now we can strike our sail, and fix
Our Sunday pennon to the mast,
Glide softly with the gliding flood
And find that all is very good.
Bravo!—great, noble man, whose fame
Will soon be far and wide related.
Bravo!—I'm moved, yet all the same
Most inexpressibly elated!
But you appear—— ?

BRAND.
               I'm suffocated.

THE MAYOR.

Pooh, a mere momentary whim!
Preach you now, till it roars again!—
Fill the folks' bushel to the brim.
Not one his wonder can contain,
The resonance is so full and plain.

BRAND.
Indeed?

THE MAYOR.
         The Dean himself is warm
In admiration and delight.

And then, what elegance of form,
And what a grandeur, what a height
In every part——

　　　　　　BRAND.
　　　　　You've noted this?

　　　　THE MAYOR.
What noted?

　　　　　BRAND.
　　　It seems great to you?

　　　　THE MAYOR.
Why, it not only seems, but is,
No matter what the point of view.

　　　　　BRAND.
It is great?　Really?　That is true——?

　　　　THE MAYOR.
Great?—yes, God bless me,—and to spare—
For folks so far to North.　Elsewhere
They've higher standards, I'm aware?
But among us who captive dwell
Amid drear wastes and barren mounds,
On the scant verge of fjord and fell,
Its greatness 'mazes and confounds.

　　　　　BRAND.
Yes, that is so, and all we do
Is,—change an old lie for a new.

　　　　THE MAYOR.
What?

　　　　　BRAND.
　　　We have lured their hearts away
From the time-honour'd gloom and mould

To soaring spire and open day.
" How venerable ! " they cried of old.
" How vast ! " in chorus now they roar—
" The like was never seen before ! "

THE MAYOR.

My worthy friend, I needs must hold
His breeding scarcely *quantum suff.*
For whom it is not great enough.

BRAND.

But clear it shall be unto all
That, as it stands, the Church is small.
To keep that hidden were to lie.

THE MAYOR.

Nay, listen,—let such whimsies fly !
What can it profit to dispraise
What you yourself have toil'd to raise ?
You've satisfied their utmost dream ;
It seems to them more rich and rare
Than aught they e'er saw anywhere :—
Let it continue so to seem !
Why should we vex their silly sight
With proffers of the flaming link,
When they're indifferent to light ?
The question's only what they think.
It does not signify a jot
Though the Church were a pigeon-cot,
If in the faith they're rooted fast,
That it is infinitely vast.

BRAND.

In every matter the same thought.

THE MAYOR.

To-day, moreover, we hold fête ;

The whole assembly is our guest;
It 'is a point of etiquette
That everything should look its best;
And for your own sake, most of all,
It were judicious to keep clear
Of that sore fact—that it is small.

BRAND.

How so?

THE MAYOR.

Well, listen, you shall hear.
Firstly, the headmen of the town
Are giving you a piece of plate,
Whose graved inscription is frustrate
If the work's size is whittled down;
And then the Ode, composed express,
And my inaugural address,—
You leave them helpless in the lurch,
Docking the greatness of the Church.
You see then, you must yield your doubt,
And boldly face the matter out.

BRAND.

I see, what oft has stung my eye,
A lying triumph crown the lie.

THE MAYOR.

But, in God's name, my worthy friend,
Where do these strong expressions tend?
However, waiving points of taste,
Hear now my second reason,—gold,
As that was silver; for, behold,
You, like a chosen son, are graced
With favour in the royal sight;
In short,—you have been named a Knight!
This very day you'll walk elate,
Cross upon breast, a titled man.

BRAND.

Another, heavier cross's weight
I bear; take that from me who can.

THE MAYOR.

What's this?　You do not seem to shake
With agitation at such prize?
You mystery of mysteries!
But pray consider, for God's sake——

BRAND.
[*Stamping.*]

This is mere babble of vain speech :—
Nothing I learn and nothing teach;
You have not grasp'd the smallest shred
Of the true sense of what I said.
I meant not greatness men compute,
And measure by the inch and foot,
But that which, viewless, darts and streams,
Pierces the soul with frosts and fires,
That beckons to impassion'd dreams,
And like the starlit heaven inspires—
That—leave me! I am worn, oppress'd ;—
Convince, teach, edify the rest.

⌊*Goes up towards the Church.*

THE MAYOR.
[*To himself.*]

In such a labyrinth who can stray
And find an issue?　Greatness lay
In something that is "viewless," "streams,"
"Not inchwise measured," "lifts to dreams,"
And "starlit heaven"?　It went so, surely?
Has he been lunching prematurely?　[*Goes.*

BRAND.

[*Comes down over the open ground.*]
So desolate on the upland drear
I never stood as I stand here ;
My impotent questionings evoke
Echoes that cackle and that croak.
　　　　[*Looks towards the* MAYOR.]
For him, I would my heel might bruise
His head!　Each time I make emprise
To loose him from the bond of lies,
With shameless wantonness he spews
His rotten soul before my eyes !—
　O Agnes, why wast thou so frail ?
Would that this hollow game were done,
Where none give in, and none prevail ;—
Yes, hopeless he that fights alone !

THE DEAN.
[*Coming up.*] *
O, my beloved !　O, my sheep—!
Nay, I beg pardon,—would have said
My reverend brother !—cannot keep
My predication from my head ;
I got it yesterday by rote,
The taste still lingers in my throat.
Enough of that.—To you I offer
My thanks, whose energy began,
Whose firmness carried through, the plan,
Despite the babbler and the scoffer ;
Fell'd that which was about to fall,
And worthily restored it all !

BRAND.

Far from that yet.

THE DEAN.

How say you, friend?
Is Consecration not the end?

BRAND.

A House new-builded asks, as well,
A cleansed Soul, therein to dwell.

THE DEAN.

All that will come without our stir.
So gay, so elegant a roof
Will be an adequate reproof
To every unwash'd worshipper.
And that delightful sounding-board,
That doubles every pious word,
Will render without fail our flocks
Fivescore per cent. more orthodox.
Results so notable as these
The first-rate Nationalities
Themselves, 'tis said, can hardly better.—
For this your Country is your debtor,
Yours only; let me then express
These heartfelt, brotherly thanks of mine,
To be re-echoed, as I guess,
In winged words across the wine,
By many a fiery young divine,
When at the festal board we crown
This the great day of your renown.—
But, my dear Brand, you look so faint—?

BRAND.

My heart and hope have long been spent.

THE DEAN.

No wonder;—with so grave a care,
And all unaided and unfriended.

But now the worst of it is ended,
And all gives promise of a splendid
Day for our function. Don't despair!
All will go well. Reflect! A throng
Has gather'd, many thousand strong,
From far-off parishes,—and who
Can vie in eloquence with you?
See where your reverend brethren stand,
To welcome you with heart and hand;
While all these lowly bosoms beat
With ardour for you, first to last!
And then, the work, so ably plann'd,
The decoration, so complete,—
The general theme—How great! How vast!
—And the unparallel'd repast!
Into the kitchen I was looking
Just now, and saw the calf a-cooking.
Nay, Brand, a pretty beast, I vow!
You must have had some trouble, now,
In these hard times, before you found
So fine a bit of flesh to cater,
With meat at half a crown a pound!
But that can be deferr'd till later.
I'm on another errand bound.

BRAND.

Speak freely; slash, stab, rive and rend!

THE DEAN.

I have a milder way, my friend.
But briefly; for our duties press.
One little matter, I confess,
I'd have you from to-day set right;
A task that cannot but be light.
Nay, I imagine you can guess
Half what I'm hinting at, at least?

I mean, your duties as a priest.
Hitherto you have been a loose
Observer still, of Wont and Use ;
But Use and Wont, if not the best
Of things, are yet the needfulest.
Well, well, I will not be severe ;
You're young, and but a novice here,
Town-bred, and scarcely understand
What country usages demand.
But now, now it is urgent, friend,
The lack of judgment to amend.
You hitherto have too much heeded
What this man and what that man needed ;
That error (in your private ear)
Is grievous.   Weigh them in the block ;
Use the same comb for all the flock ;
You won't repent it, never fear.

BRAND.

Be more explicit.

THE DEAN.
                    The thing's clear.
You for the Parish's behoof
Have built a Church.   That is the woof
That robes the spirit of Law and Peace ;
For to the State, religion is
The power that lifts and purifies,
The stronghold where its safety lies,
The universal moral measure.
You see, the State is scant of treasure,   .
And wants full value for its pence.
" Good Christians " means " good citizens."
Do you suppose it pays its pelf
To be for God and Man a tool,
And bring annoyance on itself ?

No, faith, the State is not a fool ;
And all our course would run amiss,
Did not the State, by strictest rule,
Look only to the life that is.
But the State's object, my good friend,
Through its officials must be gain'd,
In this case through its priests——

BRAND.

                              Each word
Is wisdom !   Speak !

THE DEAN.

                              I'm near the end.
This Church, you see, you have conferr'd
Upon the State, for its sole profit ;
And, therefore, all the uses of it
Must to the State's advantage tend.
This is the meaning, note it well,
Of our forthcoming celebration,
This shall be meant by chiming bell,
And this by Gift-deed's recitation.
A promise thus the Gift implies,
Whose force I'd have you scrutinise——

BRAND.
By God, I never meant it so !

THE DEAN.
Yes ; but it's now too late, you know——

BRAND.
Too late ?   Too late !   That will be seen !

THE DEAN.
Be sensible !   I can't keep grave !
What is the tragedy therein ?

You are not ask'd to promise sin ?
Souls do not grow more hard to save
Because the Country profits too ;
With due discretion and despatch
Two masters' bidding you may do ;
You were not made a priest, to snatch
Peter or Harry's single soul
Out of the torments of the lake;
But that the Parish as a whole
Might of the shower of grace partake ;
And, the whole Parish saved, it's clear,
You save every Parishioner.
The State is (what you hardly dream)
Exactly half republican :
Liberty held in strictest ban,
Equality in high esteem.
Yet is Equality never won
But by destroying More and Less,—
And it is that you have not done !
Nay, you have striven to express
And emphasise unlikenesses
That slumber'd hitherto unknown.
Men, mere Church-members till of late,
To Personalities are grown.
That does no service to the State ;
And thus it is, each Parish rate,
Each offering to the common good,
Is from unwilling niggards bled ;
The Church no longer is the hood
That fits alike on every head.

BRAND.

O, vistas infinite unfold !

THE DEAN.

Don't be cast down ; no gain in that

Though I must own I shudder at
The dire confusion I behold.
But while there's life there's hope, and you
Are by this gift baptized anew
To obligations yet more great
Of serving, by your Church, the State.
Men need a rule in all they do ;
Or reckless forces, breaking loose,
Like colts undaunted by the curb,
Spurn gates and fences, and disturb
The thousand landmarks of old Use.
Each order'd mode of life proclaims
One Law, that goes by many names.
The Artist calls it S c h o o l, and I'm
Mistaken if I have not heard
Our soldiers call it k e e p i n g t i m e.
Ah yes, friend, that's the very word !
That's what the State desires at last !
Double-quick time gets on too fast,
And goose-step lags too far behind ;
All men to step alike, and beat
The selfsame music with their feet,
That is the method to its mind !

BRAND.

Kennel the eagle ;—and let loose
On empyrean flights the goose !

THE DEAN.

We, thank the Lord, are not as these ;—
But if we must use allegory,
We'll turn to Scripture, if you please.
For every case it has a story,
From Genesis to Revelation
It swarms with stimulating Fable ;
I will but hint, in illustration,

At that projected Tower of Babe
How did the good folks prosper, pray ?
And why ? The answer's clear as day ;
Their ranks divided, sort by sort,
Each one his private language spoke,
They drew not in the common yoke,
Grew " Personalities," in short.
That's half the twofold core that lies
Embedded in this shell of fable ;—
That all strength, sever'd, is unstable,
And death-doom'd who the world defies.
When God desires a man to fall
He makes him an Original ;
The Romans had it, 'faith, that God
Made the man mad ; but mad is odd,
And oddness singleness, you know ;
Therefore who fights without a friend
Must look to suffer in the end
The fate that overtook the man
Whom David posted in the van.

BRAND.

Yes, very likely : but what though ?
In Death I see not Overthrow.
And is your faith quite firm and fast
That had those builders spoken still
One speech, and acted with one will,
They would have piled the pinnacle
Of Babel up to heaven at last ?

THE DEAN.

To heaven ? No, that is where it lies:
No man gets quite to Paradise.
There, see, we have the second core,
Embedded in this shell of fable ;—
That every building is unstable
Which to the starry heaven would soar !

BRAND.

Yet, Jacob's ladder reach'd that goal.
Thither by longing soars the Soul.

THE DEAN.

In that way! Why, God bless me, yes
Further discussion's needless there.
Heaven is the wage of faithfulness,
Of course, of moral life and prayer.
But life and faith hold such dissent,
They only thrive, when kept apart ;
Six days for toiling hands are meant,
The seventh, for stirring of the heart ;
If all the week we preach'd and pray'd,
The Sabbath had in vain been made.
God's incense, rightly to be used,
Must not be lavishly diffused ;
Worship, like Art, was not created
To be in perfume dissipated.
The Ideal you may safely sound
From pulpit's holy vantage-ground ;
But with your surplice lay it by,
When you emerge beneath the sky.
All things, as I have said, are based
On laws that strictly must be traced,
And my sole end in speaking is
To give this fact due emphasis.

BRAND.

One thing I very clearly see :
No State Soul-case is fit for me.

THE MAYOR.

A perfect fit, I will engage,
My friend,—but on a loftier stage :—
You must go up——

BRAND.

Is that an end
I reach by plunging in the mire?

THE DEAN.

Whoso him humbleth shall go higher!
Hooks will not catch, unless they bend.

BRAND.

Man can't be used, unless he perish!

THE DEAN.

Good God!　How can you think I cherish
Any such purpose?

BRAND.

Ay, indeed,
That's the condition!　First to bleed!
Your bloodless spirit to put on
Man must be first a skeleton!

THE DEAN.

I would not put the lancet through
A very kitten—far less you;
But yet I thought no harm were done
In leaving just ajar the door
That opens, where I went before.

BRAND.

And do you know what you have sought?
This, that upon the State's cock-cry
I that Ideal should deny
For which I until now have fought?

THE DEAN.

Deny, friend?　Who makes such request?
Duty is all I bid you follow:

I ask you quietly to swallow
That which your people can't digest.
Keep it intact, if you're disposed,—
But yet hermetically closed ;
At home, in God's name, soar and swell,
Not as a public spectacle ;
Trust me, the will that won't be bent
Brings its unfailing punishment.

BRAND.

Ay, fear of torment, hope of gain,
Are on thy brow the brand of Cain,
Which cries that thou by worldly art
Hast slain the Abel in thy heart !

THE DEAN.
[*To himself.*]
Upon my word he calls me " Thou " ;
That is too much !—
[*Aloud.*]
                        I will not now
Prolong our strife, but, to conclude,
Would have it clearly understood,
That if you'd prosper, you must weigh
What land you live in, and what day.
For no man wins the fight with fortune,
But in alliance with his time.
Which of the men who paint and rhyme
Dare fail when social claims importune ?
Look at our soldiers !   Why, the gleam
Of sabres is become a dream!
And wherefore ?   Since a law commands :
Postpone thy own need to the Land's !
Let each his own excrescence pare,
Neither uplift him, nor protrude,
But vanish in the multitude.

"Humane the age is," says the Mayor :
And if humanely it be met
Will bring you fame and fortune yet.
But all your angles must be rounded,
Your gnarls and bosses scraped and pounded !
You must grow sleek as others do,
All singularities eschew,
If you would labour without let.

BRAND.

Away ! away !

THE DEAN.

I quite agree.
Men of your stamp must finally
Be summon'd to a higher seat ;
But, in the greater as the less,
Only the regimental dress
Will make your happiness complete.
The corporal, staff in hand, must knock
The sense of Time into his flock ;
For, to our mind, the best of all
Commanders is the corporal.
Just as the corporal leads his men
Into the church, battalion-wise,
So must the priest lead his, again,
By parishes to Paradise.
It's all so easy !—Faith, you say,
Broad-based upon authority ;
Which, being upon learning stay'd,
May be implicitly obey'd :
While rules and ritual leave no doubt
How faith ought to be acted out.
Wherefore, my brother,—pluck up cheer !
Employ the time for meditation ;
Reflect upon your situation,
And don't give way to futile fear !

I'll see just now if I can pitch
My music to a higher note :
Though with an unaccustom'd throat,
A sounding-board's so seldom here.
Farewell, farewell !   1 mean to preach
Of human nature's sinful prime,
God's image nigh obliterated.——
But now I'm thinking it is time
The inner mortal should be baited.   [*Goes.*

BRAND
[*Stands for a moment as if petrified in thought.*]
All I have offer'd for my call,
God's as I vainly held it,——all ;
And now one trumpet-blast reveal'd
Before what idols I had kneel'd.
Not yet ! not yet !   I'm not their slave '
Yon churchyard has had blood to sup,
Light, life I've laid in yonder grave ;——
My soul shall not be yieldĕd up !
   O horrible to stand alone,——
Amid a glimmering world of dead ;
Horrible to receive a stone,
Howe'er I hunger after bread.——
   How true, how deadly true, his strain,——
But yet how vacant and how vain.
Dim broods God's dove of piercing eyes;
Alas, to me she never flies.——
O, had I but o n e faithful breast——
To give me strength, to give me rest.

EINAR, *pale, emaciated, dressed in black, comes along
the road and stops on perceiving* BRAND.

BRAND
[*Cries out.*]
.You, Einar ?

EINAR.

By that name I'm known.

BRAND.

I was just thirsting for a breast
That was not made of wood or stone !
Come, to my heart of hearts be press'd !

EINAR.

My haven's found, I am at rest.

BRAND.

You bear a grudge for the event
Of our last meeting——

EINAR.

                    In no wise ;
I blame you not.   You were but sent
To be the passive instrument
Wherewith God oped my erring eyes.

BRAND
[*starts back.*]

What tongue is this ?

EINAR.

                    The tongue of peace—
The tongue they learn, who, timely torn
From Sleep of Sin, awake new-born.

BRAND.

Marvellous ! I had heard of this,—
That you in quite another way
Were walking——

EINAR.

I was led astray
By pride, in my own strength secure.
The idols the world holds divine,
The talent I was told was mine,
My singer's voice, were all malign
Seductions unto Satan's lure.
But God (I praise Him) for me wrought,
Left not His erring sheep unsought,
He help'd me in my hour of need.

BRAND.

Help'd you—in what way ?

EINAR.

Yes, indeed :—
I fell.

BRAND.

Fell ?   How ?

EINAR.

To dissipation.
With gambling tastes He me imbued—

BRAND.

And that was God's solicitude ?

EINAR.

'Twas the first step to my salvation.
On that my health He undermined,
The talent from my fingers fled,
My love of revelry declined,
Then, to the hospital consign'd,
Long I lay sick, and round my bed
Flames seem'd to glare, and on each wall

Myriads of giant flies to crawl ;—
Came out, and soon acquaintance made
With certain sisters, three in all,
Soldiers in God's cause arm'd and paid.
And they, together with a priest,
Me from the yoke of Earth released
Pluck'd me from Sin that held me fast,
And made me the Lord's child at last.

BRAND.

Indeed ?

EINAR.

Divergent paths we follow ;
One seeks the height, and one the hollow.

BRAND.

But after ?

EINAR.

True ; I turn'd me thence,
To preach for Total Abstinence ;
But since that Work for the unwary
Is strewn with perilous temptation,
I chose another occupation,
And travel now as Missionary——

BRAND.

Where ?

EINAR.

To the Caudate-nigger State.
But now, I think, we'll separate ;
My time is precious——

BRAND.

Won't you stay ?
You see here's festival to-day.

EINAR.

Thanks, no; the swarthy Heathens wait.—
Farewell.　　　　　　　　　　　　　[*Going.*

BRAND.

And does no memory stir,
Bidding you ask— ?

EINAR.

Of what ?
BRAND.

Of her
Who would have grieved at the abyss,
That parts another day from this.

EINAR,

I guess your meaning ; you refer
To that young female, whose allure
Held me in pleasure's net secure,
Till Faith's ablution made me pure.
—Yes, and how is it then with her ?

BRAND.

Next year I won her for my wife.

EINAR.

That unimportant, I prefer
To leave these trivial facts unknown
What's weighty I desire alone.

BRAND.

God richly bless'd our common life
With joy and sorrow : The child pined——

EINAR.

That's unimportant——

BRAND.

So it is ;

He was but given to be resign'd ;
Our eyes one day shall look on his.
But afterwards she also died ;
Their graves bloom yonder side by side.

EINAR.

That's unimportant——

BRAND.

That likewise ?

EINAR.

Such things are trifles in my eyes,
How did she die, I want to know ?

BRAND.

With Hope that yet a Dawn shall glow,
With all her heart's rich treasure whole.
With Will that never lost control,
With thanks for all that life had lent
And life had taken away, she went.

EINAR.

Trumpery figments every one.
Say what the faith she died in was.

BRAND.

Unshaken.

EINAR.

In what ?

BRAND.

In God.

EINAR.

Alas

Only in Him ?   She is undone.

BRAND.

What say you ?

EINAR.

Damn'd, to my regret.

BRAND.
[*Quietly.*]

Go, scoundrel !

EINAR.

You shall feel as well
The clutches of the Lord of hell ;—
For both, eternal torments wait.

BRAND.

You, wretch, dare sentence to the Fire !
Yourself late wallow'd in the mire——

EINAR.

On me no spot is to be seen ;
The tub of Faith hath wash'd me clean ;
Each splash has vanish'd, scraped and scored
On Holiness's washing-board ;
In Vigilance's mangle I
Have wrung my Adam's-vesture dry ;
And shine like snowy surplice fair,
Soap-lather'd with the suds of Prayer !

BRAND.

Hold !

EINAR.

Hold, yourself!   Here's sulphur fume,
I see the glints of Satan's horn !
I am Salvation's good wheat-corn,
And you the shovell'd chaff of Doom.   [*Goes.*

BRAND.

[*Looks a while after him ; all at once his
     eyes flash and he breaks out.*]
That, that is the man 1 need !
Now all bonds are burst that bound me ;
Now my flag shall wave around me
Though none follow where 1 lead '

THE MAYOR.

[*Comes hastily in.*]
Pray, dear Pastor, hasten, do !
The procession-people stand
Waiting only the command—

BRAND.

Let them come then '

THE MAYOR.

           Wanting you !
Pray reflect, and hasten in !
All impatient to begin,
See, the whole mass throng and strain ;
Like a torrent after storm
On the Manse they surge and swarm,
Shouting for the Priest.   Again,
Hark you, for " the Priest " they shout,
Pray make haste !   I much misdoubt,
They may scarcely prove humane !

BRAND.

Never will I hide my face
In the crowd that you command ;
Let them seek me : here I stand.

THE MAYOR.

Are you sane ?

BRAND.

The path you pace
Is too narrow for my tread.

THE MAYOR.

And 'twill still grow less and less
As the people push ahead.
Zounds !   They spurn at rod and check !
Parsons, Dean, and Corporation
Jostled to the brimming beck— !
Quickly, friend, make application
Of the scourge of your persuasion !
Ha, too late, they smash the line ;
The procession is a wreck !

*The multitude stream in, and break in wild disorder
through the procession to the church.*

VOICES.

Priest !

OTHERS.

[*Pointing up to the Church steps, where
BRAND stands.*]
See yonder !

OTHERS AGAIN.

Give the sign !

THE DEAN.
[*Jostled in the throng.*]
Mayor, Mayor, control them, pray!

THE MAYOR.
All my words are thrown away!

THE SCHOOLMASTER.
[*To* BRAND.]
Speak to them, and cast a gleam
On their spirits' troubled stream!
What you summon'd us to see,
Was it Feast or foolery?

BRAND.
O, there stirs a current, then,
In these stagnant waters.—Men,
At the crossway stand ye : choose!
Wholly ye must will to lose
The old vesture of your lust,
Utterly anew be clad,
Ere our Temple from the dust
Rises, as it shall and must!

OFFICIALS.
He is raving!

CLERGY.
He is mad!

BRAND.
Yes, I was so, when I thought
Ye in some sense also wrought
For the God who hateth Lies!
When I dream'd that I could lure
To your hearts His Spirit pure

By a feat of compromise.
Small the Church was; logic thence
Palter'd to the inference:
Twice the size—that cannot fail;
Fivefold,—that must needs prevail!
O, I saw not that the call
Was for Nothing or else All.
Down that easy way I reel'd,
But to-day the Lord has spoken,
In this very hour has peal'd
Overhead the awful blast
Of His Judgment-trump at last,—
And I listen'd, in the wind
Of my anguish, baffled, broken,—
Even as David, having sinn'd—;
Now all hesitation dies.
Men! The Devil is compromise!

THE MULTITUDE.
[*With growing excitement.*]
Down with them that quench'd our light
Sapp'd the marrow of our might!

BRAND.
In your souls the demon dwells
That has bound you with his spells.
You have put your powers at mart,
You have cleft yourselves in twain;
Discord therefore numbs your brain,
Petrifies your hollow heart.
To the Church to-day what drew you?
But the show, the show—nought else!—
Roll of organ, clash of bells,—
And to feel the tingle through you
Of a speaking-furnace dart,

As it lisps and lilts and prattles,
As it rolls and roars and rattles,
By the strictest rules of Art !

THE DEAN.
[*To himself.*]
The Mayor's chatter, he must mean .

THE MAYOR.
[*Likewise.*]
That's the twaddle of the Dean !

BRAND.
Nothing but the altar-glow
Of the Festival you know.
Get you home then to your sloth,
Get you home to toil and stress,
Soul as well as body clothe
In its common work-day dress,—
And the Bible slumber sound
Till the next Saint's day comes round.
O, it was not to this end
That the Offering-cup I drain'd !
I the Greater Church ordain'd,
That its shadow might descend,
Not alone on Faith and Creed
But on everything in life
That by God's leave lives indeed ;—
On our daily strain and strife,
Midnight weeping, evening rest,
Youth's impetuous delight,
All that harbours of good right,
Mean or precious, in the breast.
Yonder foss's hidden thunder,
And the beck that sparkles under,
And the bellow of wild weather,

And the murmurous ocean's tongue
Should have melted, soul-possess'd,
With the organ's roll together,
And the gather'd people's song.
Sweep this lying Labour hence!
Mighty only in pretence!
Stricken inly with decay
On its consecration day,—
Symbol of your impotence.
All the germs of soul you aim
By divided toil to maim;
For the week's six days ye drag
To the deepest deep God's flag,
For one only of the seven,
Let it flutter forth to heaven!

VOICES FROM THE THRONG.

Lead us, lead us! Tempest lowers!
Lead us, and the day is ours!

THE DEAN.

Do not hear him! Nought he knows
Of the Faith a Christian owes!

BRAND.

Ay, thou nam'st the flaw whereby
Both the throng, and thou and I,
Are beset! To souls alone
Faith is possible,—show me one!
Show me one that his best treasure
Has not inly flung to waste
In his fumbling, or his haste!
First, the reeling plunge for pleasure
To the tabor's juggling strain
Till the zest of pleasure's slain;
Then, soul-ruins, charr'd and stark,

Turn to dance before the Ark!
When the cup's last liquor slips
Through the brain-worn cripple's lips,
Ho! 'tis time to pray and mend,
Sure of pardon in the end.
First God's image you outwear,
Live the beast within you bare,
Then to Mercy cry your needs,
Seeking God—as invalids!
So, His Kingdom's overthrown.
What should He with souls effete
Grovelling at His mercy-seat?
Said He not that then alone
When your lifeblood pulses tense,
Through all veins of soul and sense,
Ye His kingdom shall inherit?
Children ye must be to share it;
No man hobbles through its gate.
Come then, ye whose cheek is rife
With the bloom of childhood yet
To the greater Church of Life!

THE MAYOR.

Open it then!

THE MULTITUDE.
[*Crying out as in anguish.*]
No!   Not this!

BRAND.

It has neither mark nor bound,
But its floor the green earth is,
Mead and mountain, sea and sound;
And the overarching sky
Is its only canopy.
There shall all thy work be wrought

As an anthem for God's ear,
There thy week-day toil be sought
With no sacrilege to fear.
There the World be like a tree
Folded in its shielding bark ;
Faith and Action blended be.
There shall daily labour fuse
With right Teaching and right Use,
Daily drudgery be one
With star-flights beyond the sun,
One with Yule-tide revelry
And the Dance before the Ark.

> [*A stormy agitation passes over the multi-
> tude ; some retire ; most press close about*
> BRAND.

A THOUSAND VOICES.

Light is kindled in the dark ;—
Life and serving God's the same !

THE DEAN.

Woe on us ! He wins them—hark !
Mayor, sexton, beadle, clerk !

THE MAYOR.
> [*Aside.*]

Do not scream so, o' God's name !
With a bull who wants a bout ?
Let him roar his ravin out !

BRAND.
> [*To the multitude.*]

Hence—away ! God is afar !
Cannot be where such men are !
Fair His kingdom is and free !

> [*Locks the church-door and takes the keys
> in his hand.*]

Here I will be priest no more.
I revoke my gift ;—from me
No man shall receive the key
Of the yet unopen'd door !
    [*Throws the keys into the river.*]
Wilt thou in, thou slave of clay,—
Through the crypt-hole worm thy way ;
Lithe·thy back is, creep and ply ;
From that charnel let thy sigh
Roam the earth with venom'd breath,
Like the flagging gasp of death !

THE MAYOR.
[*Aside with relief.*]
Ha, his hope of knighthood's dim !

THE DEAN.
[*Similarly.*]
Well; no bishopric for him !

BRAND.
Come thou, young man—fresh and free—
Let a life-breeze lighten thee
From this dim vault's clinging dust.
Conquer with me !   For thou must
One day waken, one day rise,
Nobly break with compromise ;—
Up, and fly the evil days,
Fly the maze of middle ways,
Strike the foeman full and fair,
Battle to the death declare !

THE MAYOR.
Hold !   I'll read the Riot Act !

BRAND.

Read !   With you I break my pact.

THE MULTITUDE.

Show the way, and we will follow !

BRAND.

Over frozen height and hollow,
Over all the land we'll fare,
Loose each soul-destroying snare
That this people holds in fee,
Lift and lighten, and set free,
Blot the vestige of the beast,
Each a Man and each a Priest,
Stamp anew the outworn brand,
Make a Temple of the land.

> [*The multitude, including the* SEXTON *and*
> SCHOOLMASTER, *throng around him.*
> BRAND *is lifted on to their shoulders.*

MANY VOICES.

'Tis a great Time !   Visions fair
Dazzle through the noontide glare.

> [*The great mass of the assemblage streams
> away up the valley ; a few remain.*

THE DEAN.

[*To the departing crowd.*]

O, ye blinded ones, what would you ?
Lo ! behind his seeming sooth
Satan scheming to delude you !

THE MAYOR.

Ho there !   Turn !   Folks born to track
Safe home-waters still and smooth !

Stop!—ye go to ruin and wrack !—
(Dogs!   And not a word comes back !)

THE DEAN.
Think of household and of home !

VOICES FROM THE MULTITUDE.
To a greater Home we come !

THE MAYOR.
Think of meadow-plot and field ;
Think of teeming stall and fold !

VOICES.
Heavenly dews did manna yield
When the chosen starved of old !

THE DEAN.
Hark ! your women cry in chorus

VOICES.
[*In the distance.*]
Ours they are not if they quail !

THE DEAN.
" Father's gone ! " your children wail.

THE WHOLE MULTITUDE.
Be against us, or be for us !

THE DEAN.
[*Gazes a while with folded hands after them ;
then dejectedly.*]
By his faithless flock deserted
Stands the old shepherd, heavy-hearted,
Plunder'd to the very skin !

THE MAYOR.

[*Shaking his fist at* BRAND.

His the scandal; his the sin!
But we'll shortly win the fight!

THE DEAN.

[*Almost breaking down.*]

Win?　Of all our people cheated?—

THE MAYOR.

Ay, but we are not defeated,
If I know my lambs aright!

[*Follows them.*

THE DEAN.

Whither will he, in heaven's name?
As I live, he's after them!
Ha, my drooping courage rises,
I will also do and dare,—
Make assaults and capture prizes!
Bring my steed;—that is, prepare
A safe, steady mountain mare!　　　[*They go.*

---

*By the highest farms in the valley. The land rises
in the background, and passes into great barren
mountains. Rain.*
BRAND, *followed by the multitude—men, women, and
children,—comes up the slopes.*

BRAND.

Look onward!　Triumph flies ahead!
Your homes are hidden in the deep,
And over it, from steep to steep,
The storm his cloudy tent has spread.
Forget the pit of sloth ye trod,
Fly free aloft, ye sons of God!

A MAN.

Wait; my old father is dead beaten.

ANOTHER.

Since yesterday I've nothing eaten——

SEVERAL.

Ay, still our hunger, slake our thirst !

BRAND.

On, on, across the mountain first !

SCHOOLMASTER.

Which way ?

BRAND,

All ways alike are right
That reach the goal.   This way pursue——

A MAN.

Nay, it is steep, and 'twill be night
Ere we are well upon the height.

THE SEXTON.

And that way lies the Ice-church too.

BRAND.

The steep way is the short way still.

A WOMAN.

My foot is sore !

ANOTHER.

My child is ill !

A THIRD.

Where shall I get a drop to drink ?

THE SCHOOLMASTER.
Priest, feed the people ;—see, they sink.

MANY VOICES.
A miracle !   A miracle !

BRAND.
O, the slave-stamp has branded deep;
The toil you shirk, the hire you crave.
Up, and shake off this deadly sleep,—
Or else, get back into the grave !

THE SCHOOLMASTER.
Ay, he is right; first face the foe ;
The hire comes afterwards, you know.

BRAND.
It shall, as sure as God looks forth
Over the breadth and depth of Earth !

MANY VOICES.
He's prophesying!   He's prophesying

SEVERAL.
Hark, priest, will it be warm, this fight ?

OTHERS.
And bloody ?   And will it last till night ?

THE SCHOOLMASTER.
[*Asiue.*]
I trust there is no risk of dying ?

A MAN.
Priest, must we really face the fire ?

ANOTHER.

What is my portion of the hire ?

A WOMAN.

You're sure I shall not lose my son ?

THE SEXTON.

By Tuesday will the field be won ?

BRAND.

[*Looking round in bewilderment on the throng.*]
What would you know? What's your demand?

THE SEXTON.

Firstly, how long we shall make war.
Then, of our total loss therein.
And finally,—how much we win ?

BRAND.

This ye demand ?

THE SEXTON.

          Yes, 'faith ; before
We did not rightly understand.

BRAND.

[*Deeply moved.*]
Then ye shall understand it now !

THE MULTITUDE.

[*Thronging closer.*]
Speak !   Speak !

BRAND.

          How long the war will last?
As long as life, till ye have cast

All ye possess before the Lord,
And slain the Spirit of Accord;
Until your stiff will bend and bow,
And every coward scruple fall
Before the bidding ¿ Nought or All !
What you will lose ?   Your gods abhorr'd,
Your feasts to Mammon and the Lord,
The glittering bonds ye do not loathe,
And all the pillows of your sloth !
What you will gain ?   A will that's whole,—
A soaring faith, a single soul,
The willingness to lose, that gave
Itself rejoicing to the grave ;—
A crown of thorns on every brow ;—
That is the wage you're earning now !

THE MULTITUDE.
[*With a furious cry.*]

Betray'd !   Betray'd !   Deceived !   Misled !

BRAND.

I say but what I always said !

SEVERAL.

You promised us the victor's prize ;
And now it turns to sacrifice !

BRAND

I promised victory,—and to you
Victory shall indeed be due.
But every man who fights in front
Must perish in the battle's brunt ;
If that he dares not, let him lay
His arms down ere the battle-day
The flag's predestined to surrender
That has a timorous defender ;

And he that shudders at the cost,
Ere he is wounded, he is lost.

THE MULTITUDE.

He insolently bids us die
To serve unborn posterity!

BRAND.

Through thorny steeps of sacrifice,
The way unto our Canaan lies.
Triumph through death!   I call you all,
As Champions of God to fall!

THE SEXTON.

Well, we are in a pretty plight!
No mercy to expect below——

THE SCHOOLMASTER.

Nay, we have bade the dale good-night.

THE SEXTON.

And forward, forward, who will go?

SOME.

To death with him!

THE SCHOOLMASTER.

                    'Twere pity, so!
We want a general, you know!

WOMEN.

[Pointing in terror downwards.]
The Dean!   The Dean!

THE SCHOOLMASTER.

[To the throng.]
                    Nay, never fear!

The Dean.

[*Comes in, followed by some of those who
remained behind.*]
O my beloved ! O my sheep !
To the old shepherd's voice give ear !

The Schoolmaster.

[*To the throng.*]
A home no more we have below ;
Better we follow up the steep !

The Dean.

That ye could grieve my heart so sore,
And pierce me with a wound so deep !

Brand.

Thou wast their soul's scourge evermore !

The Dean.

Don't heed him ! He is stuffing you
With idle promises.   ∘

Several.

That's true !

The Dean.

But we are gracious, and forgive
Where we true penitence perceive.
O, turn your eyes into your hearts
And mark the diabolic arts
With which he won you to his aid !

The Multitude.

Ay, sure enough ; we were betray'd !

The Dean.

And then consider ; what can ye,

A knot of scatter'd dalesmen, do ?
Are high heroic deeds for you ?
Can ye give bondsmen liberty ?
You have your daily task ; pursue it !
Whatever is beyond, eschew it !
What can your prowess brave or baulk ?
Ye have your humble homes to keep.
What would you between eagle and hawk ?
What would you between wolf and bear ?
Ye fall but to the strongest's share.
O my beloved !   O my sheep !

THE MULTITUDE.

Ay, woe on us,—his words are true !

THE SEXTON.

And yet, when from the dale we drew,
Upon ourselves we locked the door ;
We have no home there, as before.

THE SCHOOLMASTER.

No, he has open'd all our eyes,
Laid bare sins, sicknesses, and lies ;
The sleepy people sleeps no more ;
And deadly to our waking seems
The life that satisfied our dreams.

THE DEAN.

Ah, trust me, that will soon pass over.
All will return to the old state,
If you will just be still and wait.
These folks, I'll wage, will soon recover
The wonted calm they have foregone.

BRAND.

Choose, men and women !

SOME.

Home !

OTHERS.

Too late !

Too late !　Along the height press on !

THE MAYOR.
[*Enters in haste.*]
O lucky chance I caught you up

WOMEN.
Ah, dear kind master, don't be stern

THE MAYOR.
Not now; provided you return !
A better day, a brighter season
Dawns for us !　If you'll hark to reason,
You'll all be rich men ere you sup !

SEVERAL.
How so ?

THE MAYOR.
There is a herring-horde
By millions swimming in the fjord !

THE MULTITUDE.
What does he say ?

THE MAYOR.
Set all to rights !
Fly from these stormy uplands bare.
Till now the herrings swam elsewhere ;
Now, friends, at last, our barren bights
Good fortune tardily requites.

BRAND.

Between God's summons choose, and his!

THE MAYOR.

Consult your own shrewd faculties!

THE DEAN.

A Miracle Divine is here!
A Providential Token clear!
How oft I dreamt that this befell!
I took it for a nightmare's spell;
And now its meaning is revealed——

BRAND.

Yourselves you ruin, if you yield!

MANY.

A herring-horde!

THE MAYOR.

By millions told!

THE DEAN.

For wife and children, bread and gold!

THE MAYOR.

You see, then, this is not an hour
To waste your forces in a fray,
And against energies whose power
Strikes in the very Dean dismay.
Now ye have other ends in view
Than idly pining for the sky.
Heaven, trust me, can your arms defy,
And God's not easy to subdue.
Don't mix yourselves in others' strife,
But gather in the proffer'd fruit,

That is a practical pursuit,
That does not call for blood and knife ;
That asks no sacrifice of life,
And gives you its good things to boot !

BRAND.

Just sacrifice is His demand,—
Flame-writ in Heaven by His hand !

THE DEAN.

Ah, if you feel a call that way,
Just come to me next Sunday, say,
And on my word I'll——

THE MAYOR.
[*Interrupting.*]
　　　　　　　Yes, yes, yes !

THE SEXTON.
[*Aside to the* DEAN.]
Shall I be suffer'd keep my place ?

THE SCHOOLMASTER.
[*Similarly.*]
Shall I be forced to leave my school ?

THE DEAN.
[*Aside to them.*]
If these stiff necks you overrule
We will deal mildly with your case.

THE MAYOR.

Away—away with you ! time flies !

THE SEXTON.

To boat, to boat, whoever's wise !

SOME.

A y, but the priest ?————

THE SEXTON.

O, leave the fool !

THE SCHOOLMASTER.

Here speaks the Lord as clearly, look,
As in an open printed book !

THE MAYOR.

Leave him ; that's law and justice too ;
With babbling tales he flouted you.

SEVERAL.

He lied to us !

THE DEAN.

His creed's accursed ;
And think, he never got a First !

SOME.

Never got what ?

THE MAYOR.

A grain of sense.

THE SEXTON.

Nay, of that we have evidence !

THE DEAN.

Vainly his mother's dying breath
For the last sacrament made suit !

THE MAYOR.

His child he almost did to death !

THE SEXTON.

His wife as well!

WOMEN.

O heartless brute!

THE DEAN.

Bad spouse, bad father, and bad son,—
Worse Christian surely there is none!

MANY VOICES.

Our ancient Church he overthrew!

OTHERS.

And shot the bolt upon the new!

OTHERS AGAIN.

He wreck'd us in a roaring stream!

THE MAYOR.

He pilfer'd my Asylum-scheme!

BRAND.

On every branded brow I see
This generation's destiny.

THE WHOLE THRONG.
[*Roaring.*]

Hoo, never heed him!   Stone and knife!
Send the fiend flying for his life!
        [BRAND *is driven with stones out into the wild.*
        His pursuers then return.

THE DEAN.

O my beloved!   O my sheep!
Back to your homes and hearths once more;

Your eyes in true repentance steep,
And see what blessings are in store.
God in His mercy is so good,
He asketh not the guiltless blood ;—
And our authorities as well
Are singularly placable ;
Mayor, magistrate, and sheriff too,
Will not be over hard on you ;
And for myself, that large humanity
That marks our modern Christianity
Is mine ; your rulers will descend
And dwell with you, as friend with friend.

THE MAYOR.

But should abuses be detected,
They must, past question, be corrected.
When we've a little time to move,
I'll have appointed a commission,
To seek how best we may improve
Your intellectual condition.
Some clergymen it should include
Such as the Dean and I think good,—
And furthermore, if you prefer,
The Sexton and the Schoolmaster,
With others of a humbler sort,—
You'll all be satisfied, in short.

THE DEAN.

Yes, we'll relieve your burdens all,
As ye this day have brought relief
To your old shepherd in his grief.
Let each find comfort in the thought
That here a miracle was wrought.
Farewell ! Good fortune to your haul !

THE SEXTON.

Ah, there's true charity, if you will !

THE SCHOOLMASTER.

So meek and unassuming still.

WOMEN.

So kindly, and so nice !

OTHER WOMEN.

And then
Such condescending gentlemen !

THE SEXTON.

They don't demand the martyr's throe.

THE SCHOOLMASTER.

The Lord's Prayer is not all they know.
[*The throng passes on downwards.*

THE DEAN.
[*To the* MAYOR.]
Ah, that has taken.   It is plain
A great revulsion is in train ;
For, by God's blessed benefaction,
There is a thing men call Reaction.

THE MAYOR.

'Twas my achievement, to control
The infant riot ere it grew.

THE DEAN.

Ah, to the miracle most was due.

THE MAYOR.

What miracle ?

THE DEAN.
The herring-shoal.

THE MAYOR.
[*Whistling.*]
That was, I need not say, a lie.

THE DEAN.
Really, a lie?

THE MAYOR.
I just let loose
At the first fancy that came by;
Is it a sin such means to use
In such a cause?

THE DEAN.
God bless me, no
Need is an adequate excuse.

THE MAYOR.
And then, to-morrow, when the glow
Of agitation's dead, or dying,
What will it matter if the end
Was gain'd by telling truth, or lying?

THE DEAN.
I am no formalist, my friend.
[*Looks up into the wild.*]
But is't not Brand that yonder drags
His slow course upward?

THE MAYOR.
Ay, you're right!
A lonely warrior off to fight!

THE DEAN.
Nay, there's another too—that lags
Far in the rear!

THE MAYOR.
　　　Why ;—that is Gerd ;
The herdsman's worthy of the herd.

THE DEAN,
[*Facetiously.*]
When he has still'd his losing whim,
This is the epitaph for him :
" Here lieth Brand ; his tale's a sad one ;
One soul he saved,—and that a mad one !"

THE MAYOR.
[*With his finger to his nose.*]
But, on reflection, I have some
Misgivings that the folk's decree
A little lack'd humanity.

THE DEAN.
[*Shrugging his shoulders.*]
Vox populi vox Dei.　　Come !

　　　　　　　　　　　　　[*They go*

*High up among the mountains. A storm is rising and
chasing the clouds heavily over the snow-slopes ;
black peaks and summits appear here and there,
and are veiled again by the mist.*
BRAND *comes, bleeding and broken, up the mountain.*

BRAND.
[*Stops and looks backward.*]
From the vale they follow'd thronging,
Never one has reached the height.
Through all bosoms thrill'd the longing
For a greater Day's dawn-light ;

Through all souls subduing strode
The alarum-call of God.
But the sacrifice they dread!
Will, the weakling, hides his head;—
One man died for them of yore,—
Cowardice is crime no more!
[*Sinks down on a stone, and looks with shrinking
gaze around.*]
Oft I shudder'd at their doom;
And I walk'd, with horror quivering,
As a little child walks shivering
Amid shrieking shapes that loom
In a dim and haunted room.
But I check'd my bosom's quaking,
And bethought me, and consoled it:
Out of doors the day is breaking,
Not of night it is, this gloom,
But the shutters barr'd enfold it;
And I thought, the day inwelling,
Rich with summer's golden bloom,
Shall anon prevail, expelling
All the darkness that is dwelling
In the dim and haunted room.
    O how bitter my dismay!
Pitchy darkness on me broke,—
And, without, a nerveless folk
Sat forlorn by fjord and bay,
Dim traditions treasuring
While their sotted souls decay.
Even as, year by year, the king
Treasured up his Snefrid dead,
Loosed the linen shroud o'erspread
By her mute heart listening low,
Still upon hope's fragments fed,
Thinking, "*Now* the roses red
In her pallid ashes blow!"

None, like him, arose, and gave
The grave's debt unto the grave ;
None among them wise to know :
" Dreaming cannot kindle dust,
Down into the earth it must,
Dust is only made to breed
Nurture for the new-sown seed."
Night, black night,—and night again
Over children, women, men !
O could I with levin-flame
Save them from the straw-death's shame !
　　　　　　[*Leaps up.*]
　Gloomy visions I see sweep
Like the Wild Hunt through the night.
Lo, the Time is Tempest-dight,
Calls for heroes, death to dare,
Calls for naked steel to leap,
And for scabbards to hang bare ;—
Kinsfolk, lo, to battle riding,
While their gentle brothers, hiding,
From the hat of darkness peep.
And yet more I do divine—
All the horror of their shame,—
Men that shriek and wives that whine,
Deaf to every cry and claim,
See them on their brows imprinting
" Poor folks sea-bound " for their name,
" Humble farthings of God's minting ! "
Pale they listen to the fray,—
Willing-weakness for their shield.—
Rainbow o'er the mead of May,
Flag, where fliest thou now afield ?
Where's that tricolor to-day,—
Which the wind of myriad song,
Beat and bellied from the mast
Till a zealot king at last

Split it into teeth and tongue?
But you used the tongue to brag;
And what boots the toothed flag
If the dragon dares not bite?
Would the folk had spared those cheers,
And the zealot king those shears!
Four-square flag of peace suffices,
When a stranded craft capsizes,
To give warning of her plight!
   Direr visions, worse foreboding,
Glare upon me through the gloom!
Britain's smoke-cloud sinks corroding
On the land in noisome fume;
Smirches all its tender bloom,
All its gracious verdure dashes,
Sweeping low with breath of bane,
Stealing sunlight from the plain,
Showering down like rain of ashes
On the city of God's doom.—
Fouler featured men are grown;—
Dropping water's humming drone
Echoes through the mine's recesses:
Bustling, smug, a pigmy pack
Plucks its prey from ore's embraces,
Walks with crooked soul and back,
Glares like dwarfs with greedy eyes
For the golden glittering lies;
Speechless souls with lips unsmiling,
Hearts that fall of brothers rends not,
Nor their own to fury frets,
Hammer-wielding, coining, filing;
Light's last gleam forlornly flies;
For this bastard folk forgets
That the need of willing ends not
When the power of willing dies!
   Direr visions, direr doom,

Glare upon me through the gloom.
Craft, the wolf, with howl and yell,
Bays at Wisdom, sun of earth ;
Cries of ruin ring to North,
Call to arms by fjord and fell ;
And the pigmy, quaking, grim,
Hisses : " What is that to him ? "
Let the other nations glow,
Let the mighty meet the foe,
We can ill afford to bleed,—
We are weak, may fairly plead
From a giants' war exemption,
Need not offer All as meed
For our fraction of Redemption.
Not for us the cup He drank,
Not for us the thorny wreath
In His temples drove its teeth,
Not for us the spear-shaft sank
In the Side whose life was still.
Not for us the burning thrill
   Of the nails that clove and tore.
   We, the weak, the least accounted,
   Battle-summons may ignore !
Not for us the Cross He mounted !
Just the stirrup-slash's stain,
Just the gash the cobbler scored
In the shoulder of the Lord,
Is our portion of His pain !
   [*Throws himself down in the snow and covers
      his face ; presently he looks up.*]
Was I dreaming ! Dream I still ?
Mist-enshrouded is the hill.
Were those visions but the vain
Phantoms of a fever'd brain ?
Is the image clean outworn
Whereunto Man's soul was born ?

Is the Maker's spirit fled——
[*Listening.*]
Ha, what song breaks overhead?

INVISIBLE CHOIR.
[*In the sough of the storm.*]
Never shalt thou win His spirit;
Thou in mortal flesh wast born:
Spurn his bidding or revere it;
Equally thou art forlorn.

BRAND.
[*Repeats the words, and says softly.*]
Woe's me, woe; I well may fear it!
Stood He not, and saw me pray,
Sternly smote my prayer away?
All I loved He has demanded,
All the ways of light seal'd fast,
Made me battle single-handed,
And be overthrown at last!

THE CHOIR.
[*Louder, above him.*]
Worm, thou mayst not win His spirit,—
For Death's cup thou hast consumed;
Fear His Will, or do not fear it,
Equally thy work is doom'd.

BRAND.
[*Softly.*]
Agnes, Alf, the gladsome life
When unrest and pain I knew not—
I exchanged for tears and strife,
In my own heart plunged the knife,—
But the fiend of evil slew not.

THE CHOIR.
[*Tender and alluring.*]
Dreamer, thine is not His spirit,
Nought to Him thy gifts are worth;
Heaven thou never shalt inherit,
Earth-born creature, live for Earth!

BRAND.
[*Breaks into soft weeping.*]
Alf and Agnes, come unto me!
Lone I sit upon this peak!
Keen the north wind pierces through me,
Phantoms seize me, chill ones, meek———!

*He looks up ; a glimmering space opens and clears in
the mist ; the* APPARITION *of a* WOMAN *stands in
it, brightly clad, with a cloak over its shoulders.
It is* AGNES.

THE PHANTOM.
[*Smiles, and spreads its arms towards him.*]
See, again, Brand, I have found thee!

BRAND.
[*Starting up in bewilderment.*]
Agnes! Agnes! What is this?

THE PHANTOM.
Dearest, it is thy release
From the fever'd dreams that bound thee!

BRAND.
Agnes! Agnes!
                    [*He is hurrying towards her.*

THE PHANTOM.
[*Screams.*]
                    Cross not !   Deep
Rolls between us the abyss,
Where the mountain-torrents sweep !
[*Tenderly.*]
Thou dost dream not, neither sleep,
Nor with phantoms wagest war ;
Dear, by sickness thou wast wasted,—
Frenzy's bitter cup hast tasted,
Dreamt, thy wife had fled afar.

BRAND.
Oh, thou livest !   Blessed be——— !

THE PHANTOM.
[*Hastily.*]
Peace !   Of that no murmur now !
Follow fast, the moments press.

BRAND.
Oh, but Alf !

THE PHANTOM.
Alive, no less.

BRAND.
Lives '

THE PHANTOM.
                    And with unfaded brow '
All thy sorrows did but seem !
All thy battles were a dream,
Alf is with thy mother ; she
Vigorous yet, and stalwart he ;
Still the old Church stands entire ;
Pluck it down if thou desire ;—

And the dalesmen still drudge on
As they did in good days gone.

BRAND.

" Good ! "

THE PHANTOM.
For days of peace they were.

BRAND.

" Peace ? "

THE PHANTOM.
O haste thee, Brand, O fly !

BRAND.

Woe, I dream !

THE PHANTOM.
Thy dream's gone by,
But thou needest sheltering care——

BRAND.

I am strong.

THE PHANTOM.
Ah me, not yet;
Still the fell dream lies in wait.
Once again from wife and child
It shall sweep thee, cloud-beguiled,
Once again thy soul obscure,—
If thou wilt not seek the cure.

BRAND.

Oh, vouchsafe it !

THE PHANTOM.
Thou availest,
Thou alone, that cure to reach.

BRAND.

Name it then!

THE PHANTOM.

The aged leech,
Who has conn'd so many a page,—
The unfathomably sage,
He discovered where thou ailest.
All the phantoms of thy strife,
Three words conjured them to life.
Them thou boldly must recall,
From thy memory efface them,
From thy conscience blot, erase them;
At their bidding, lo, thou burnest
In this maddening blast of bane;—
O forget them, if thou yearnest
To make white thy soul again!

BRAND.

Say, what are they?

THE PHANTOM.

Nought or all.

BRAND.

[*Reeling back.*]

Is it so?

THE PHANTOM.

So sure as I
Am alive, and thou wilt die.

BRAND.

Woe on us! The sword once more
Swings above us, as before!

THE PHANTOM.

Brand, be kind; my breast is warm;

Clasp me close in thy strong arm ;—
Let us fly where summer's sun——

BRAND.

Never more that plague shall bind me.

THE PHANTOM.

Ah, Brand, all is not yet won.

BRAND.

[*Shaking his head.*]
I have flung that dream behind me.
Me no more that phantom-strife's
Horror thrills ;—but Life's ! but Life's !

THE PHANTOM.

Life's ?

BRAND.

Come, Agnes, where I lead !

THE PHANTOM.

Brand, what is it thou wilt do ?

BRAND.

What I must : the dream make true,—
Live the vision into deed.

THE PHANTOM.

Ha, thou canst not !   Think but whither
That road led thee.

BRAND.

Thither ! Thither !

THE PHANTOM.

What thou dared'st, dream-beguiled,
Wilt thou, whole and waking, dare ?

BRAND.

Whole and waking.

THE PHANTOM.
Lose the child ?

BRAND.

Lose it.

THE PHANTOM.
Brand !

BRAND.
I must.

THE PHANTOM.
And tear
Me all bleeding from the snare ?
With the rods of sacrifice
Scourge me to the death ?

BRAND.
I must

THE PHANTOM.
Quench the glow of sunny skies,
Turn all bright things into dust,
Never pluck life's fruitage fair,
Never be upborne by song ?
Ah, so many memories throng !

BRAND.
Nought avails.   Lose not thy prayer.

THE PHANTOM.
Heed'st thou not thy martyr's meed ?
Baffled where thou sought'st to waken,
Stoned by all, by all forsaken ?

BRAND.

Not for recompense I bleed;
Not for trophies do I fight.

THE PHANTOM.

For a race that walks entomb'd

BRAND.

One to many can give light.

THE PHANTOM.

All their generation's doom'd.

BRAND.

Much availeth one will's might.

THE PHANTOM.

" One " with fiery sword of yore
Man of Paradise bereft !
At the gate a gulf he cleft ;—
Over that thou mayst not soar !

BRAND.

But the path of yearning's left

THE PHANTOM.

[*Vanishes in a thunder-clap ; the mist fills the place
where it stood ; and a piercing scream is heard,
as of one flying.*]
Die ! Earth cannot use thee more !

BRAND.

[*Stands a moment in bewilderment.*]
Out into the mist it leapt,—
Plumy wings of falcon beating,

Down along the moorland swept.
For a finger it was treating,
That the hand might be its prize—!
Ha, the Spirit of Compromise !

GERD.

[*Comes with a rifle.*]
Hast thou seen the falcon ?

BRAND.
                              Yea ;
This time I have seen him.

GERD.
                              Say,
Quick, which way thou saw'st him fly ;
We will chase him, thou and I.

BRAND.
Steel and bullet he defies ;
Oftentimes you think he flies
Stricken by the mortal lead,—
But draw near to strike him dead,
Up he starts again, secure,
With the old cajoling lure.

GERD.
See, the hunter's gun I've got,
Steel and silver is the shot ;
'Trow, my wits are less astray
Than they reckon '

BRAND.
            Have thy way .
                              [*Going.*

GERD.

Priest, thou walkest lame afoot.

BRAND.

I was hunted.

GERD.

Red thy brow
As the blood of thy heart's root !

BRAND.

I was beaten.

GERD.

Musical
Was thy voice of old, that now
Rattles like the leaves of Fall.

BRAND.

I was———

GERD.

What ?

BRAND.

By one and all

Spurn'd.

GERD.
[*Looking at him with great eyes.*]
Aha,—I know thee now !
For the priest I took thee ;—pest
Take the priest and all the rest !
The One, greatest Man art thou !

BRAND.

So I madly dared to trust.

GERD.

Let me look upon thy hands !

BRAND.

On my hands ?

GERD.

They're pierced and torn !
In thy hair the blood-dew stands,
Riven by the fanged thorn
In thy forehead fiercely thrust,
Thou the crucifix didst span !
In my childhood Father told me
'Twas another, long ago,
Far away, that suffer'd so ;—
Now I see he only fool'd me ;—
Thou art the Redeeming man !

BRAND.

Get thee hence !

GERD.

Shall I not fall
Low before thy feet and pray ?

BRAND.

Hence !

GERD.

Thou gavest the blood away
That hath might to save us all !

BRAND.

Oh, no saving plank I see,
In my own soul's agony !

GERD.

Take the rifle   Shoot them dead—

BRAND.

[*Shaking his head.*]
Man must struggle till he falls.

GERD.

Oh, not thou; thou art the head!
By the nails thy hands were gored;—
Thou art chosen; thou art Lord.

BRAND.

I'm the meanest worm that crawls.

GERD.

[*Looks up; the clouds are lifting.*]
Know'st thou where thou stand'st?

BRAND.

[*Gazing before him.*]
                             Below
The first step of the ascent;
It is far, and I am faint.

GERD.

[*More fiercely.*]
Say! Where art thou, dost thou know?

BRAND.

Yes, now falls the misty shroud.

GERD.

Yes, it falls: without a cloud
Svartetind impales the blue!

BRAND.

[*Looking up.*]
Svartetind? The ice-church

GERD.
Yea!
Here thou camest churchward, too!

BRAND.

Hence! a thousand miles away!—
How I long to fly afar,
Where the sunlight and the balm
And the holy hush of calm,
And Life's summer-kingdoms are!
[*Bursts into tears.*]
Jesus, I have cried and pleaded,—
From thy bosom still outcast;
Thou hast pass'd me by unheeded
As a well-worn word is passed;
Of salvation's vesture, stain'd
With the wine of tears unfeign'd,
Let me clasp one fold at last!

GERD.
[*Pale.*]
What is this? Then weepest, thou,
Hot tears, till thy cheek is steaming,—
And the glacier's death-shroud streaming
Silently from crag and crest,—
And my memory's frozen tides
Melt to weeping in my breast,—
And the snowy surplice glides
Down the Ice-priest's giant sides—
[*Trembling.*]
Man, why wept'st thou not till now?

BRAND.
[*Radiant, clear, and with an air of renewed youth.*]
Through the Law an ice-track led,—
Then broke summer overhead!
Till to-day I strove alone

To be God's pure tablet-stone ;—
From to-day my life shall stream
Lambent, glowing, as a dream.
The ice-fetters break away,
I can weep,—and kneel,—and pray !

[Sinks upon his knees.

GERD.

*[Looks askance upwards, and then, softly and
timidly.]*

There he sits, the ugly sprite !
'Tis his shadow sweeps the land,
Where he flogs the mountain height
With his flapping vans in flight.
Now Redemption is at hand——
If the silver will but bite !

*[Puts the rifle to her cheek and shoots. A
hollow roar, as of distant thunder, is
heard far up the precipice.*

BRAND.

[Starting up.]

Ha, what dost thou ?

GERD.

Down he slides !

I have hit him ;—down he swings,—
Shrieking, till the echo rings ;
Plumes in thousand from his sides
Flutter down the beetling brae ;—
See how large he looms, how white—]
Ha, he's rolling down this way !

BRAND.

[Sinking down.]

Blood of children must be spilt
To atone the parent's guilt !

GERD.

Tenfold vaster at his fall
Grew the tent of Heaven above!
See him tumble; see him sprawl—!
Ah, I will not shudder more;
He is white, see, as a dove—!
[Shrieks in terror.]
Hu, the horrible thunder-roar!
[Throws herself down in the snow.

BRAND.

*[Crouches under the descending avalanche, and,
looking up, speaks.]*
God, I plunge into death's night,—
Shall they wholly miss thy Light
Who unto man's utmost might
Will'd—?
*[The avalanche buries him; the whole valley
is swallowed up.*

A VOICE.

[Calls through the crashing thunder.]
He is the God of Love.

THE END.

PRINTED BY
BALLANTYNE & COMPANY LTD
AT THE BALLANTYNE PRESS
TAVISTOCK STREET COVENT GARDEN
LONDON

ImTheStory.com

Personalized Classic Books in many genre's

Unique gift for kids, partners, friends, colleagues

Customize:

- Character Names
- Upload your own front/back cover images (optional)
- Inscribe a personal message/dedication on the
  inside page (optional)

Customize many titles Including
- Alice in Wonderland
- Romeo and Juliet
- The Wizard of Oz
- A Christmas Carol
- Dracula
- Dr. Jekyll & Mr. Hyde
- And more...

CPSIA information can be obtained at www.ICGtesting.com
Printed in the USA
BVOW04s1012100614

355951BV00023B/1136/P